CISM EXAM PASS

CERTIFIED INFORMATION SECURITY MANAGER STUDY GUIDE

4 BOOKS IN 1

BOOK 1
CISM EXAM PREP: FOUNDATION PRINCIPLES AND CONCEPTS

BOOK 2
MASTERING RISK MANAGEMENT IN INFORMATION SECURITY FOR CISM

BOOK 3
ADVANCED STRATEGIES FOR GOVERNANCE AND COMPLIANCE IN CISM

BOOK 4
EXPERT TECHNIQUES FOR INCIDENT RESPONSE AND DISASTER RECOVERY IN CISM

ROB BOTWRIGHT

Published by Rob Botwright
Library of Congress Cataloging-in-Publication Data
ISBN 978-1-83938-791-3
Cover design by Rizzo

Disclaimer

The contents of this book are based on extensive research and the best available historical sources. However, the author and publisher make no claims, promises, or guarantees about the accuracy, completeness, or adequacy of the information contained herein. The information in this book is provided on an "as is" basis, and the author and publisher disclaim any and all liability for any errors, omissions, or inaccuracies in the information or for any actions taken in reliance on such information. The opinions and views expressed in this book are those of the author and do not necessarily reflect the official policy or position of any organization or individual mentioned in this book. Any reference to specific people, places, or events is intended only to provide historical context and is not intended to defame or malign any group, individual, or entity. The information in this book is intended for educational and entertainment purposes only. It is not intended to be a substitute for professional advice or judgment. Readers are encouraged to conduct their own research and to seek professional advice where appropriate. Every effort has been made to obtain necessary permissions and acknowledgments for all images and other copyrighted material used in this book. Any errors or omissions in this regard are unintentional, and the author and publisher will correct them in future editions.

BOOK 1 - CISM EXAM PREP: FOUNDATION PRINCIPLES AND CONCEPTS

BOOK 2 - MASTERING RISK MANAGEMENT IN INFORMATION SECURITY FOR CISM

BOOK 3 - ADVANCED STRATEGIES FOR GOVERNANCE AND COMPLIANCE IN CISM

BOOK 4 - EXPERT TECHNIQUES FOR INCIDENT RESPONSE AND DISASTER RECOVERY IN CISM

Introduction

Welcome to the "CISM Exam Pass" book bundle, your comprehensive study guide for achieving success in the Certified Information Security Manager (CISM) exam. This bundle is designed to equip aspiring CISM professionals with the knowledge, skills, and strategies needed to excel in the field of information security management.

Book 1: "CISM Exam Prep: Foundation Principles and Concepts," lays the groundwork for your CISM journey by providing a comprehensive overview of the foundational principles and concepts of information security management. From understanding the core domains of the CISM exam to mastering essential concepts such as information security governance and risk management, this book serves as your starting point in building a solid foundation for success.

Book 2: "Mastering Risk Management in Information Security for CISM," delves deep into the intricacies of risk management within the context of information security. From risk assessment methodologies to developing effective risk mitigation strategies, this book provides readers with the tools and techniques needed to navigate the complex landscape of cybersecurity risks and threats.

Book 3: "Advanced Strategies for Governance and Compliance in CISM," takes your knowledge to the next level by exploring advanced strategies for governance and compliance in information security management. From emerging trends to best practices, this book empowers readers to develop robust governance frameworks and ensure compliance with regulatory requirements.

Book 4: "Expert Techniques for Incident Response and Disaster Recovery in CISM," equips readers with the expertise needed to effectively respond to and recover from cybersecurity incidents and disasters. From incident response methodologies to advanced forensic techniques, this book provides readers with the skills and strategies needed to handle incidents and disasters with agility and precision.

Together, the books in the "CISM Exam Pass" bundle offer a comprehensive and structured approach to preparing for the CISM exam. Whether you're looking to enhance your knowledge, advance your career, or obtain professional certification, this bundle serves as your ultimate guide on your journey towards becoming a Certified Information Security Manager. Let's embark on this journey together and unlock the doors to a rewarding career in information security management.

BOOK 1
CISM EXAM PREP
FOUNDATION PRINCIPLES AND CONCEPTS

ROB BOTWRIGHT

Chapter 1: Introduction to Information Security Management

Information security fundamentals are essential for safeguarding sensitive data and preventing unauthorized access to critical systems. Understanding the basics of information security is paramount in today's interconnected digital landscape. It encompasses various principles, practices, and technologies aimed at protecting data integrity, confidentiality, and availability. One of the foundational concepts in information security is the CIA triad, which stands for confidentiality, integrity, and availability. Confidentiality ensures that data is only accessible to authorized users or entities, protecting it from unauthorized disclosure. Integrity ensures that data remains accurate and unaltered, guarding against unauthorized modification or tampering. Availability ensures that data and resources are accessible when needed, minimizing downtime and ensuring continuity of operations. These principles guide the design and implementation of security measures to mitigate risks and threats effectively. In addition to the CIA triad, other fundamental concepts include authentication, authorization, and accountability. Authentication verifies the identity of users or entities, ensuring that only legitimate users gain access to resources. Authorization determines the permissions and privileges granted to authenticated users, defining what actions they can perform within a system or network. Accountability holds users accountable for their actions by logging and monitoring their activities, enabling traceability and auditability. These concepts form the basis of access control mechanisms, such as role-based access control (RBAC) and mandatory access control (MAC), which enforce security policies and enforce least privilege principles. Encryption is another fundamental technique used to protect data confidentiality and integrity. It involves encoding plaintext data into ciphertext using cryptographic algorithms and keys, rendering it unreadable to unauthorized parties. Encryption is commonly used to secure data transmissions over networks, store sensitive information in databases, and protect data at rest on storage devices. Techniques such as symmetric encryption, where the same key is used for both encryption and decryption, and asymmetric encryption, where a public-private key pair is used, are employed to secure data in different scenarios. Key management is crucial in encryption to ensure the secure generation, distribution, and storage of cryptographic keys. Secure key management practices help prevent unauthorized access to encrypted data and mitigate the risk of key compromise. In addition to encryption, organizations deploy various security controls and technologies to protect their assets and mitigate risks. Firewalls, intrusion detection systems (IDS), and intrusion prevention systems (IPS) are used to monitor and filter network traffic, detect and prevent unauthorized access, and defend against cyber threats. Endpoint security solutions, such as antivirus software and host-based intrusion detection systems (HIDS), are deployed to protect individual devices from malware and unauthorized access. Security information and event management (SIEM) systems are employed to centralize logging, monitor security events, and facilitate incident response and forensic investigations. Security awareness and training programs are essential for promoting a culture of security within organizations. Educating employees about security best practices, such as creating strong passwords, recognizing phishing attempts, and reporting security incidents, helps mitigate the human factor in security breaches. Regular security assessments, such as vulnerability scanning and penetration testing, are conducted to identify and remediate security vulnerabilities proactively. Compliance with industry regulations and standards, such as the General Data Protection Regulation (GDPR) and the Payment Card Industry Data Security Standard (PCI DSS), is essential for ensuring the protection of sensitive data and maintaining trust with customers and stakeholders. Implementing a robust security governance framework, which includes policies, procedures, and oversight mechanisms, helps organizations establish accountability and responsibility for information security at all levels. Continuous monitoring and evaluation of security controls and practices are necessary to adapt to evolving threats and vulnerabilities. By incorporating these fundamental principles and practices into their security posture, organizations can strengthen their defenses, mitigate risks, and protect their valuable assets from cyber threats. Information security management plays a critical role in protecting organizations from cyber threats and safeguarding sensitive data from unauthorized access, alteration, or disclosure. In today's digital age, where businesses rely heavily on technology for their operations, the importance of information security management cannot be overstated. It encompasses a comprehensive approach to identifying, assessing, and mitigating security risks to ensure the confidentiality, integrity, and availability of information assets. Effective information security management requires a combination of policies, procedures, technologies, and awareness programs tailored to the organization's specific needs and risk profile. One of the key aspects of information security management is risk management, which involves identifying potential threats and vulnerabilities to the organization's information assets and implementing controls to mitigate those risks. Risk management encompasses various activities, including risk assessment, risk treatment, and risk monitoring, to ensure that security measures are aligned with business objectives and regulatory requirements. Conducting regular risk assessments helps organizations identify and prioritize security risks based on their likelihood and potential impact on business operations. Techniques such as vulnerability scanning, penetration testing, and threat modeling are commonly used to assess security risks and vulnerabilities in systems, networks, and applications. Once risks are identified, organizations can implement risk treatment measures to mitigate or eliminate them. This may involve implementing technical controls such as firewalls, intrusion detection systems, and encryption to protect against external threats, as well as administrative controls such as security policies, procedures, and training to address internal risks. Continuous monitoring and review of security controls are essential to ensure their effectiveness and adaptability to changing threats and vulnerabilities. Another important aspect of information security management is compliance with regulatory requirements and industry standards. Many industries have specific regulations and standards governing the protection of sensitive information, such as the Health Insurance Portability and Accountability Act (HIPAA) for healthcare organizations and the Payment Card Industry Data Security Standard (PCI DSS) for businesses that handle payment card data. Compliance with these regulations is not only a legal requirement but also helps organizations demonstrate their commitment to protecting customer data and maintaining trust with stakeholders. Information security management also encompasses incident response and management, which involves detecting, responding to, and recovering from security incidents such as data breaches, malware infections, and denial-of-service attacks. Having an effective incident response plan in place is crucial for minimizing the impact of security incidents and restoring normal operations quickly. This involves establishing incident response teams, defining roles and responsibilities, and developing procedures for incident detection, containment, eradication, and recovery. Incident response plans should be regularly tested and updated to ensure their effectiveness in addressing evolving threats and vulnerabilities. In addition to protecting against external threats, information security management also addresses insider threats, which can pose significant risks to organizations. Insider threats may include malicious insiders who intentionally misuse or abuse their access privileges, as well as negligent insiders who inadvertently compromise security through careless actions such as clicking on phishing links or mishandling sensitive data. Implementing access controls, monitoring user activity, and providing security awareness training can help mitigate the risk of insider threats. Ultimately, information security management is not just a technology issue but a business issue that requires the involvement and cooperation of all stakeholders within an organization. It requires a proactive and holistic approach that considers the organization's overall risk profile, business objectives, and regulatory requirements. By prioritizing information security management and investing in robust security measures, organizations can protect their valuable assets, maintain trust with customers and stakeholders, and achieve their business goals in an increasingly digital world.

Chapter 2: Understanding the CISM Certification

The CISM (Certified Information Security Manager) certification is a globally recognized credential that validates the expertise of information security professionals in managing and overseeing enterprise information security programs. It is offered by ISACA (Information Systems Audit and Control Association) and is designed for individuals who are responsible for developing, implementing, and managing information security initiatives within their organizations. The CISM certification is highly regarded in the field of information security and is often considered a prerequisite for senior-level positions in the industry. To earn the CISM certification, candidates must meet certain eligibility requirements and pass the CISM exam, which assesses their knowledge and skills across four domains: Information Security Governance, Information Risk Management, Information Security Program Development and Management, and Information Security Incident Management. Each domain covers specific knowledge areas and tasks that are essential for effective information security management. The Information Security Governance domain focuses on establishing and maintaining a framework for information security governance, including defining roles and responsibilities, aligning information security with business objectives, and ensuring compliance with legal and regulatory requirements. It also covers topics such as developing and implementing information security policies, standards, and procedures, and establishing metrics and key performance indicators (KPIs) to measure the effectiveness of information security initiatives. The Information Risk Management domain addresses the identification, assessment, and mitigation of information security risks within the organization. It includes tasks such as conducting risk assessments, analyzing risk factors, and developing risk mitigation strategies and plans. It also covers topics such as risk communication and reporting, risk monitoring and control, and integrating risk management into the overall business risk management process. The Information Security Program Development and Management domain focuses on the design, implementation, and management of information security programs that align with organizational goals and objectives. It includes tasks such as developing information security strategies and roadmaps, establishing security awareness and training programs, and managing security projects and initiatives. It also covers topics such as resource allocation and budgeting, vendor management, and performance measurement and reporting. The

Information Security Incident Management domain covers the planning, response, and recovery phases of managing information security incidents within the organization. It includes tasks such as developing incident response plans and procedures, establishing incident detection and reporting mechanisms, and coordinating incident response activities across the organization. It also covers topics such as conducting post-incident reviews and lessons learned sessions, and implementing corrective actions to prevent future incidents. In addition to passing the CISM exam, candidates must also adhere to ISACA's Code of Professional Ethics and agree to comply with the Continuing Professional Education (CPE) policy to maintain their certification. This requires earning a minimum number of CPE credits each year through activities such as attending training courses, participating in professional development activities, and contributing to the profession through speaking engagements or publications. ISACA also offers various resources and study materials to help candidates prepare for the CISM exam, including review courses, practice exams, and study guides. Additionally, candidates may choose to supplement their preparation with self-study resources, such as books, online courses, and study groups. Once certified, CISM professionals can pursue a wide range of career opportunities in information security management, including roles such as Chief Information Security Officer (CISO), Information Security Manager, Security Consultant, and Risk Manager. The CISM certification is recognized and respected by employers worldwide and can provide professionals with a competitive edge in the job market. Overall, the CISM certification offers information security professionals the knowledge, skills, and credibility they need to excel in their careers and make a positive impact on their organizations' security posture. The CISM (Certified Information Security Manager) certification offers numerous benefits and career opportunities for information security professionals looking to advance their careers and demonstrate their expertise in managing and overseeing information security programs. One of the primary benefits of obtaining the CISM certification is the validation of one's knowledge and skills in information security management, which is recognized and respected by employers worldwide. The certification demonstrates a commitment to excellence in information security and provides professionals with a competitive edge in the job market. Additionally, earning the CISM certification can lead to increased job opportunities and higher earning potential. According to the Global Knowledge IT Skills and Salary Report, professionals with the CISM certification earn an average salary of over $120,000 per year, making it one of the highest-paying certifications in the field of information security. Furthermore, the CISM certification opens doors to senior-level positions in information security management, such as Chief Information Security Officer (CISO), Information Security Manager, Security Consultant, and Risk Manager. These roles offer greater responsibility, influence, and leadership opportunities within organizations, as well as the ability to shape and execute information security strategies that align with business objectives. Another benefit of the CISM certification is the opportunity for professional growth and development. ISACA, the organization that administers the CISM certification, offers various resources and networking opportunities for certified professionals to stay updated on the latest trends, best practices, and industry developments in information security management. This includes access to conferences, seminars, webinars, and online forums where professionals can share knowledge, exchange ideas, and build relationships with peers and industry experts. Additionally, maintaining the CISM certification requires earning Continuing Professional Education (CPE) credits each year, which encourages ongoing learning and development and ensures that certified professionals stay current with evolving technologies and trends in information security. The CISM certification also provides professionals with a comprehensive understanding of information security governance, risk management, program development and management, and incident management, which are critical skills for addressing the complex challenges and threats facing organizations today. This knowledge not only enhances job performance but also enables professionals to make informed decisions, mitigate risks, and effectively communicate with stakeholders at all levels of the organization. Furthermore, the CISM certification is globally recognized and respected by employers, government agencies, and industry organizations, making it a valuable credential for professionals seeking opportunities to work internationally or in highly regulated industries such as finance, healthcare, and government. The certification demonstrates proficiency in implementing and managing information security programs that comply with industry standards and regulatory requirements, such as the General Data Protection Regulation (GDPR), the Health Insurance Portability and Accountability Act (HIPAA), and the Payment Card Industry Data Security Standard (PCI DSS). This can be particularly advantageous for professionals seeking roles in organizations that handle sensitive information or have stringent security and compliance requirements. Additionally, the CISM certification provides professionals with the knowledge and skills to effectively communicate and collaborate with stakeholders across the organization, including executives, business leaders, IT professionals, and external partners. This is essential for gaining buy-in and support for information security initiatives, aligning security objectives with business goals, and fostering a culture of security awareness and accountability. Overall, the CISM certification offers numerous benefits and career opportunities for information security professionals seeking to advance their careers, demonstrate their expertise, and make a meaningful impact on their organizations' security posture. By earning the CISM certification, professionals can enhance their credibility, expand their job prospects, and contribute to the success and resilience of their organizations in an increasingly digital and interconnected world.

Chapter 3: Fundamentals of Information Security Governance

Governance structures play a crucial role in organizations by providing a framework for decision-making, accountability, and oversight across all levels of the organization. These structures define the roles, responsibilities, and relationships between key stakeholders, including executives, management, employees, and external partners. Effective governance structures help ensure that the organization's objectives are aligned with its mission, vision, and values, and that resources are allocated efficiently to achieve desired outcomes. There are various types of governance structures, each with its own characteristics and benefits. One common type of governance structure is the hierarchical or top-down structure, where decision-making authority flows from the top of the organization down to lower levels. In this structure, executives and senior management have the authority to make strategic decisions and set policies and objectives for the organization, while middle managers and employees are responsible for implementing these decisions and carrying out day-to-day operations. Another type of governance structure is the decentralized or flat structure, where decision-making authority is distributed across multiple levels of the organization. In this structure, employees are empowered to make decisions within their areas of responsibility, leading to greater autonomy and flexibility in decision-making. Decentralized governance structures are often found in agile organizations or those that value innovation and creativity. Matrix structures are another common type of governance structure, where employees report to both functional managers and project managers, resulting in a dual reporting relationship. This structure allows organizations to leverage expertise and resources across functional areas and projects, but it can also lead to complexity and challenges in coordination and communication. Regardless of the type of governance structure, effective communication and collaboration are essential for success. This involves establishing clear channels of communication, fostering a culture of transparency and openness, and ensuring that all stakeholders have access to the information they need to make informed decisions. In addition to defining decision-making authority and responsibilities, governance structures also establish mechanisms for accountability and oversight. This includes defining performance metrics and key performance indicators (KPIs) to measure progress towards goals and objectives, conducting regular performance reviews and evaluations, and implementing mechanisms for feedback and continuous improvement. Governance structures also play a critical role in risk management by establishing processes and controls to identify, assess, and mitigate risks to the organization. This includes defining risk appetite and tolerance levels, establishing risk management frameworks and methodologies, and implementing controls to monitor and manage risks effectively. For example, organizations may use risk registers to document and track risks, risk assessments to evaluate the likelihood and impact of risks, and risk mitigation plans to address identified risks. Governance structures also help ensure compliance with legal and regulatory requirements by establishing policies, procedures, and controls to ensure that the organization operates in accordance with applicable laws, regulations, and standards. This includes establishing compliance frameworks, conducting regular compliance audits and assessments, and implementing corrective actions to address non-compliance issues. For example, organizations may use compliance management software to automate compliance processes, track regulatory changes, and ensure that policies and procedures are up to date and effective. In addition to internal governance structures, organizations may also be subject to external governance requirements imposed by regulatory bodies, industry associations, or other stakeholders. This may include requirements related to financial reporting, data privacy and security, environmental sustainability, or corporate social responsibility. Compliance with these external governance requirements is essential for maintaining trust and credibility with stakeholders and avoiding legal and reputational risks. Overall, governance structures play a critical role in organizations by providing a framework for decision-making, accountability, and oversight. Effective governance structures help ensure that the organization operates efficiently and effectively, achieves its objectives, and manages risks appropriately. By defining roles, responsibilities, and relationships, governance structures enable organizations to align resources, manage performance, and comply with legal and regulatory requirements, ultimately contributing to long-term success and sustainability. The role of governance in information security is paramount for ensuring the confidentiality, integrity, and availability of organizational data and systems, as well as for managing risks and complying with legal and regulatory requirements. Governance provides the structure, processes, and oversight mechanisms necessary to establish and maintain effective information security programs. It encompasses various activities, including defining policies and procedures, allocating resources, assigning responsibilities, and monitoring performance, to ensure that information security objectives are aligned with business goals and objectives. One of the key functions of governance in information security is to establish a framework for decision-making and accountability within the organization. This involves defining roles and responsibilities for key stakeholders, such as executives, management, IT staff, and employees, and establishing mechanisms for oversight and review to ensure that information security policies and procedures are followed and that resources are allocated appropriately. Governance also helps ensure that information security initiatives are aligned with business objectives and priorities, enabling organizations to prioritize investments and allocate resources effectively to address the most critical security risks and vulnerabilities. For example, organizations may use risk-based approaches to prioritize security initiatives, focusing on the areas of highest risk or potential impact to the business. Governance also plays a critical role in managing risks related to information security by establishing processes and controls to identify, assess, and mitigate risks effectively. This includes defining risk management frameworks and methodologies, conducting risk assessments, and implementing controls to manage identified risks. For example, organizations may use risk registers to document and track risks, risk assessments to evaluate the likelihood and impact of risks, and risk mitigation plans to address identified risks. Governance also helps ensure compliance with legal and regulatory requirements related to information security by establishing policies, procedures, and controls to ensure that the organization operates in accordance with applicable laws, regulations, and standards. This includes establishing compliance frameworks, conducting regular compliance audits and assessments, and implementing corrective actions to address non-compliance issues. For example, organizations may use compliance management software to automate compliance processes, track regulatory changes, and ensure that policies and procedures are up to date and effective. Governance also helps foster a culture of security awareness and accountability within the organization by promoting the importance of information security and encouraging employees to take responsibility for protecting sensitive information and systems. This includes providing training and awareness programs to educate employees about security risks and best practices, as well as establishing mechanisms for reporting security incidents and concerns. For example, organizations may use phishing simulations to test employees' awareness of phishing threats and provide targeted training to address any gaps identified. Governance also plays a critical role in incident response and management by establishing processes and procedures for detecting, responding to, and recovering from security incidents. This includes defining incident response plans and procedures, establishing incident detection and reporting mechanisms, and coordinating incident response activities across the organization. For example, organizations may use incident response playbooks to document predefined response procedures for different types of incidents and conduct regular incident response exercises to test the effectiveness of their response plans and procedures. In summary, the role of governance in information security is multifaceted and essential for ensuring that organizations effectively manage risks, comply with legal and regulatory requirements, and protect sensitive information and systems from cyber threats. By establishing clear policies, procedures, and controls and fostering a culture of security awareness and accountability, governance enables organizations to achieve their information security objectives and safeguard their valuable assets in an increasingly digital and interconnected world.

Chapter 4: Principles of Risk Management in Information Security

Identifying risks in information security is a critical step in protecting an organization's sensitive data and systems from potential threats and vulnerabilities. It involves identifying and assessing potential risks that could compromise the confidentiality, integrity, or availability of information assets and implementing controls to mitigate those risks effectively. One common approach to identifying risks in information security is to conduct a risk assessment, which involves systematically analyzing the organization's assets, threats, vulnerabilities, and potential impacts to determine the likelihood and potential impact of various risks. A risk assessment typically consists of several key steps, including identifying assets, identifying threats and vulnerabilities, assessing the likelihood and potential impact of risks, and prioritizing risks for mitigation. To identify assets, organizations must first understand what information assets they have and where they are located. This includes identifying both digital assets, such as data stored on servers, databases, and cloud services, and physical assets, such as servers, networking equipment, and mobile devices.

Organizations may use asset inventory tools and databases to document and track their assets and dependencies. Once assets are identified, organizations can then identify potential threats and vulnerabilities that could pose risks to those assets. Threats are potential events or circumstances that could cause harm to an organization's information assets, while vulnerabilities are weaknesses or deficiencies in the organization's security controls that could be exploited by threats. Common threats to information security include malware infections, phishing attacks, insider threats, and natural disasters, while vulnerabilities may include unpatched software, weak passwords, misconfigured systems, and inadequate access controls. Organizations may use threat modeling techniques, such as brainstorming sessions, threat intelligence feeds, and historical incident data, to identify potential threats and vulnerabilities relevant to their specific environment and industry. Once threats and vulnerabilities are identified, organizations can then assess the likelihood and potential impact of various risks to their information assets. Likelihood refers to the probability that a specific threat will exploit a vulnerability and cause harm to an organization's assets, while potential impact refers to the extent of harm that could result from a successful attack. Organizations may use qualitative or quantitative risk assessment methods to assess the likelihood and potential impact of risks, depending on their resources and capabilities. Qualitative risk assessment methods involve assigning subjective ratings or scores to risks based on expert judgment or predefined criteria, while quantitative risk assessment methods involve using mathematical models and statistical analysis to estimate the likelihood and potential impact of risks based on historical data or empirical evidence. Once risks have been assessed, organizations can then prioritize risks for mitigation based on their likelihood and potential impact. This involves identifying which risks pose the greatest threat to the organization's information assets and which risks are most urgent or critical to address. Organizations may use risk matrices or risk scoring models to prioritize risks based on predefined criteria, such as severity, likelihood, and impact. Once risks have been identified and prioritized, organizations can then implement controls to mitigate those risks effectively. This may involve implementing technical controls, such as firewalls, antivirus software, encryption, and intrusion detection systems, to prevent or detect unauthorized access, malware infections, and other security threats. It may also involve implementing administrative controls, such as security policies, procedures, and training programs, to educate employees about security risks and best practices and ensure compliance with security policies and regulations. Additionally, organizations may implement physical controls, such as access controls, surveillance cameras, and alarms, to protect physical assets from theft, vandalism, or unauthorized access. Regardless of the type of controls implemented, organizations must regularly monitor and review their security posture to ensure that controls are effective in mitigating risks and that new risks are identified and addressed promptly. This may involve conducting regular security assessments, vulnerability scans, penetration tests, and security audits to identify weaknesses and vulnerabilities in the organization's security controls and procedures. It may also involve monitoring security logs, alerts, and incident reports for signs of suspicious activity or security breaches and responding to incidents and breaches promptly to minimize the impact on the organization's information assets and reputation. In summary, identifying risks in information security is a critical process that involves systematically analyzing an organization's assets, threats, vulnerabilities, and potential impacts to determine the likelihood and potential impact of various risks. By conducting risk assessments, organizations can identify and prioritize risks for mitigation and implement controls to protect their information assets effectively. Regular monitoring and review of the organization's security posture are essential for maintaining a strong security posture and responding to new and emerging threats effectively. Risk assessment techniques are essential tools for organizations to identify, analyze, and prioritize risks to their information assets and systems effectively. These techniques help organizations understand their risk exposure and develop strategies to mitigate potential threats and vulnerabilities. One common risk assessment technique is the qualitative risk assessment method, which involves assigning subjective ratings or scores to risks based on expert judgment or predefined criteria. This method is often used when quantitative data is limited or unavailable and relies on the knowledge and experience of risk assessors to evaluate the likelihood and potential impact of risks. To conduct a qualitative risk assessment, organizations typically use risk matrices or risk scoring models to assess the likelihood and potential impact of various risks based on predefined criteria, such as severity, likelihood, and impact. Risks are then prioritized for mitigation based on their scores, with higher scores indicating greater severity or likelihood. Another risk assessment technique is the quantitative risk assessment method, which involves using mathematical models and statistical analysis to estimate the likelihood and potential impact of risks based on historical data or empirical evidence. This method is often used when quantitative data is available and provides a more objective and data-driven approach to risk assessment. To conduct a quantitative risk assessment, organizations may use techniques such as scenario analysis, Monte Carlo simulation, or fault tree analysis to estimate the likelihood and potential impact of various risks based on probabilistic models and data inputs. Risks are then prioritized for mitigation based on their estimated probabilities and potential impacts, with higher probabilities or impacts indicating greater severity or likelihood. In addition to qualitative and quantitative risk assessment methods, organizations may also use hybrid risk assessment methods that combine elements of both qualitative and quantitative approaches. Hybrid risk assessment methods offer the flexibility to incorporate subjective judgment and expert opinion while also leveraging quantitative data and analysis techniques to enhance the accuracy and reliability of risk assessments. For example, organizations may use a risk assessment matrix that combines qualitative risk scoring with quantitative data inputs to provide a more comprehensive and nuanced assessment of risks. Regardless of the risk assessment technique used, organizations must follow a systematic process to ensure that risks are identified, analyzed, and prioritized effectively. This process typically involves several key steps, including identifying assets, identifying threats and vulnerabilities, assessing the likelihood and potential impact of risks, and prioritizing risks for mitigation. To identify assets, organizations must first understand what information assets they have and where they are located. This includes identifying both digital assets, such as data stored on servers, databases, and cloud services, and physical assets, such as servers, networking equipment, and mobile devices. Organizations may use asset inventory tools and databases to document and track their assets and dependencies. Once assets are identified, organizations can then identify potential threats and vulnerabilities that could pose risks to those assets. Threats are potential events or circumstances that could cause harm to an organization's information assets, while vulnerabilities are weaknesses or deficiencies in the organization's security controls that could be exploited by threats. Common threats to information security include malware infections, phishing attacks, insider threats, and natural disasters, while vulnerabilities may include unpatched software, weak passwords, misconfigured systems, and inadequate access controls. Organizations may use threat modeling techniques, such as brainstorming sessions, threat intelligence feeds, and historical incident data, to identify potential threats and vulnerabilities relevant to their specific environment and industry. Once threats and vulnerabilities are identified, organizations can then assess the likelihood and potential impact of various risks to their information assets. Likelihood refers to the probability that a specific threat will exploit a vulnerability and cause harm to an organization's assets, while potential impact refers to the extent of harm that could result from a successful attack. Organizations may use qualitative or quantitative risk assessment methods to assess the likelihood and potential impact of risks, depending on their resources and capabilities. Qualitative risk assessment methods involve assigning subjective ratings or scores to risks based on expert judgment or predefined criteria, while quantitative risk assessment methods involve using mathematical models and statistical analysis to estimate the likelihood and potential impact of risks based on historical data or empirical evidence. Once risks have been assessed, organizations can then prioritize risks for mitigation based on their likelihood and potential impact. This involves identifying which risks pose the greatest threat to the organization's information assets and which risks are most urgent or critical to address. Organizations may use risk matrices or risk scoring models to prioritize risks based on predefined criteria, such as severity, likelihood, and impact. Once risks have been identified and prioritized, organizations can then implement controls to mitigate those risks effectively. This may involve implementing technical controls, such as firewalls, antivirus software, encryption, and intrusion detection systems, to prevent or detect unauthorized access, malware infections, and other security threats. It may also involve implementing administrative controls, such as security policies, procedures, and training programs, to educate employees about security risks and best practices and ensure compliance with security policies and regulations. Additionally, organizations may implement physical controls, such as access controls, surveillance cameras, and alarms, to protect physical assets from theft, vandalism, or unauthorized access. Regardless of the type of controls implemented, organizations must regularly monitor and review their security posture to ensure that controls are effective in mitigating risks and that new risks are identified and addressed promptly. This may involve conducting regular security assessments, vulnerability scans, penetration tests, and security audits to identify weaknesses and vulnerabilities in the organization's security controls and procedures. It may also involve monitoring security logs, alerts, and incident reports for signs of suspicious activity or security breaches and responding to incidents and breaches promptly to minimize the impact on the organization's information assets and reputation. In summary, identifying risks in information security is a critical process that involves systematically analyzing an organization's assets, threats, vulnerabilities, and potential impacts to determine the likelihood and potential impact of various risks. By conducting risk assessments, organizations can identify and prioritize risks for mitigation and implement controls to protect their information assets effectively. Regular monitoring and review of the organization's security posture are essential for maintaining a strong security posture and responding to new and emerging threats effectively.

Chapter 5: Key Concepts in Information Security Incident Management

The incident management process is a crucial component of an organization's overall cybersecurity strategy, providing a structured approach for detecting, responding to, and recovering from security incidents effectively. This process involves several key steps, including incident detection, triage, investigation, containment, eradication, recovery, and post-incident analysis, each aimed at minimizing the impact of security incidents and restoring normal operations as quickly as possible. Incident management begins with incident detection, which involves monitoring network traffic, system logs, and security alerts for signs of suspicious or malicious activity. Organizations may use intrusion detection systems (IDS), intrusion prevention systems (IPS), security information and event management (SIEM) tools, and endpoint detection and response (EDR) solutions to detect and alert on security incidents in real-time. Once an incident is detected, it must be triaged to determine its severity and potential impact on the organization's systems and data. This involves assessing the scope and nature of the incident, identifying affected assets, and prioritizing response efforts accordingly. Incident triage may involve gathering additional information about the incident, such as the type of attack, the systems or applications targeted, and the extent of the compromise. Organizations may use incident response playbooks or decision trees to guide the triage process and ensure that incidents are prioritized and addressed appropriately. Following incident triage, organizations must conduct a thorough investigation to determine the root cause of the incident and identify any vulnerabilities or weaknesses in their systems or controls that may have contributed to the incident. This may involve analyzing network traffic, system logs, and forensic evidence to reconstruct the sequence of events leading up to the incident and identify indicators of compromise (IOCs) or attack patterns. Incident investigations may also involve collaborating with internal teams, such as IT, security operations, and legal, as well as external partners, such as law enforcement agencies, forensic investigators, and incident response consultants. Once the incident has been investigated, organizations must take immediate action to contain the incident and prevent further damage or unauthorized access to their systems and data. This may involve isolating affected systems or networks, disabling compromised user accounts or credentials, and implementing temporary security controls or restrictions to limit the spread of the incident. Organizations may use network segmentation, firewall rules, access control lists (ACLs), and other network security measures to contain the incident and prevent lateral movement by attackers. After containment, organizations must focus on eradicating the incident and removing all traces of malware or unauthorized access from their systems and networks. This may involve removing malicious files or processes, patching vulnerabilities or misconfigurations, and restoring affected systems or data from backups. Organizations may use antivirus software, malware removal tools, and vulnerability scanners to identify and remediate security issues and ensure that their systems are secure and compliant with security best practices. Following eradication, organizations must focus on recovery and restoring normal operations as quickly as possible. This may involve restoring backups, rebuilding compromised systems, and implementing additional security measures to prevent future incidents. Organizations may use disaster recovery plans, business continuity plans, and incident response playbooks to guide the recovery process and ensure that critical systems and services are restored in a timely manner. Finally, organizations must conduct a post-incident analysis to evaluate their incident response efforts, identify lessons learned, and make improvements to their incident management processes and controls. This may involve conducting a root cause analysis to identify the underlying causes of the incident, documenting incident response activities and outcomes, and updating incident response playbooks or procedures based on lessons learned. Organizations may also use incident response metrics and key performance indicators (KPIs) to measure the effectiveness of their incident response efforts and identify areas for improvement. In summary, the incident management process is a critical component of an organization's cybersecurity strategy, providing a structured approach for detecting, responding to, and recovering from security incidents effectively. By following a systematic process for incident detection, triage, investigation, containment, eradication, recovery, and post-incident analysis, organizations can minimize the impact of security incidents and restore normal operations quickly and efficiently.

Incident classification and response levels are crucial aspects of an organization's incident management process, providing a framework for categorizing and prioritizing security incidents based on their severity and potential impact. Incident classification involves assigning a severity level or category to each incident based on its characteristics, such as the type of attack, the systems or data affected, and the potential impact on the organization's operations. This helps organizations prioritize response efforts and allocate resources effectively to address the most critical incidents first. One common approach to incident classification is the use of incident response categories, such as critical, high, medium, and low, to categorize incidents based on their severity and potential impact. Critical incidents are those that pose a significant threat to the organization's systems, data, or operations and require immediate attention and escalation to senior management or executive leadership. Examples of critical incidents may include data breaches, network outages, or ransomware attacks that disrupt critical systems or services and have the potential to cause widespread damage or financial loss. High-priority incidents are those that pose a serious threat to the organization's systems, data, or operations and require prompt action and escalation to management or IT security teams for investigation and remediation. Examples of high-priority incidents may include malware infections, phishing attacks, or unauthorized access attempts that compromise sensitive information or pose a risk to data confidentiality or integrity. Medium-priority incidents are those that pose a moderate threat to the organization's systems, data, or operations and require attention and follow-up by IT or security teams to investigate and address the incident appropriately. Examples of medium-priority incidents may include suspicious network traffic, system performance issues, or policy violations that warrant further investigation or monitoring to determine the root cause and potential impact. Low-priority incidents are those that pose a minimal threat to the organization's systems, data, or operations and may be addressed through routine procedures or automated responses without significant impact on business operations or security posture. Examples of low-priority incidents may include routine security alerts, software vulnerabilities, or minor policy violations that can be resolved quickly and easily without disrupting normal operations. In addition to incident classification, organizations must also establish response levels or tiers to define the level of response and resources allocated to each incident based on its severity and potential impact. Response levels typically range from Level 1 to Level 4, with Level 1 representing the lowest severity and Level 4 representing the highest severity. At Level 1, incidents are typically routine or minor in nature and can be resolved quickly and easily through standard procedures or automated responses. These incidents may not require escalation or involvement from senior management or specialized teams and can be handled by frontline IT or security staff. At Level 2, incidents are more significant in nature and may require additional resources or expertise to investigate and address effectively. These incidents may involve more complex or sophisticated attacks, such as advanced malware or targeted phishing campaigns, that require specialized tools or techniques to detect and mitigate. At Level 3, incidents are critical or high-priority in nature and require immediate attention and escalation to senior management or executive leadership for resolution. These incidents may involve serious threats to the organization's systems, data, or operations that require coordination with internal teams, external partners, or law enforcement agencies to address effectively. At Level 4, incidents are catastrophic or existential in nature and pose a severe threat to the organization's survival or reputation. These incidents may involve major data breaches, widespread network outages, or sophisticated cyberattacks that require a full-scale emergency response and crisis management plan to mitigate and recover from effectively. In summary, incident classification and response levels are essential components of an organization's incident management process, providing a structured framework for categorizing and prioritizing security incidents based on their severity and potential impact. By classifying incidents appropriately and establishing response levels or tiers, organizations can ensure that incidents are addressed promptly and effectively, minimizing the impact on business operations and protecting sensitive information and systems from potential threats and vulnerabilities.

Chapter 6: Overview of Information Security Program Development

Information security programs consist of various components, each playing a crucial role in protecting an organization's sensitive data and systems from potential threats and vulnerabilities. One essential component of an information security program is security policies and procedures, which provide the foundation for defining and implementing security controls and practices across the organization. These policies and procedures establish guidelines and requirements for protecting sensitive information, managing access to systems and data, and responding to security incidents effectively. Examples of security policies may include data classification and handling policies, access control policies, and incident response policies, while procedures may include password management procedures, data encryption procedures, and security awareness training programs. Another key component of information security programs is risk management, which involves identifying, assessing, and mitigating risks to the organization's information assets and systems. Risk management activities may include conducting risk assessments, identifying threats and vulnerabilities, and implementing controls to mitigate identified risks effectively. Organizations may use risk management frameworks, such as ISO 27001 or NIST SP 800-30, to guide their risk management efforts and ensure that risks are identified, assessed, and managed systematically. Vulnerability management is another critical component of information security programs, focusing on identifying and remediating vulnerabilities in the organization's systems and applications before they can be exploited by attackers. Vulnerability management activities may include scanning systems for known vulnerabilities, prioritizing vulnerabilities based on their severity and potential impact, and implementing patches or other security updates to address identified vulnerabilities. Organizations may use vulnerability scanning tools, such as Nessus or Qualys, to identify vulnerabilities in their systems and applications and prioritize remediation efforts accordingly. Incident response is another essential component of information security programs, providing a structured approach for detecting, responding to, and recovering from security incidents effectively. Incident response activities may include incident detection and triage, investigation and analysis, containment and eradication, recovery and restoration, and post-incident analysis and lessons learned. Organizations may use incident response playbooks, incident response teams, and incident response tools, such as SIEM solutions or forensic analysis tools, to facilitate their incident response efforts and ensure that incidents are addressed promptly and effectively. Security awareness training and education are also critical components of information security programs, helping to educate employees about security risks and best practices and promote a culture of security awareness and accountability throughout the organization. Security awareness training programs may include online courses, classroom training sessions, phishing simulations, and security awareness campaigns to educate employees about common security threats, such as phishing attacks, malware infections, and social engineering scams, and teach them how to recognize and respond to these threats appropriately. Compliance and governance are additional components of information security programs, focusing on ensuring that the organization complies with relevant laws, regulations, and industry standards and adheres to internal policies and procedures. Compliance and governance activities may include conducting regular compliance audits and assessments, documenting and reporting compliance status, and implementing controls to address identified compliance gaps or deficiencies. Organizations may use compliance management software, such as RSA

Archer or MetricStream, to automate compliance processes and ensure that policies and procedures are followed consistently across the organization. Finally, continuous monitoring and improvement are essential components of information security programs, focusing on monitoring the effectiveness of security controls and practices and identifying opportunities for improvement. Continuous monitoring activities may include monitoring network traffic, system logs, and security alerts for signs of suspicious activity or security breaches, conducting regular security assessments and penetration tests, and reviewing incident response metrics and KPIs to identify areas for improvement. Organizations may use security information and event management (SIEM) solutions, intrusion detection and prevention systems (IDS/IPS), and security analytics tools to facilitate continuous monitoring efforts and ensure that security controls are effective in mitigating risks and protecting sensitive information and systems from potential threats and vulnerabilities. In summary, information security programs consist of various components, including security policies and procedures, risk management, vulnerability management, incident response, security awareness training, compliance and governance, and continuous monitoring and improvement, each playing a crucial role in protecting an organization's sensitive data and systems from potential threats and vulnerabilities. By implementing a comprehensive information security program that addresses these components effectively, organizations can minimize the risk of security breaches and data loss and ensure the confidentiality, integrity, and availability of their information assets and systems. Planning and implementing security programs is a critical aspect of protecting an organization's sensitive data and systems from potential threats and vulnerabilities, requiring careful consideration of various factors and the implementation of appropriate controls and practices. One of the first steps in planning and implementing a security program is conducting a comprehensive risk assessment to identify and prioritize security risks and vulnerabilities that could pose a threat to the organization's information assets and systems. This involves assessing the likelihood and potential impact of various risks, such as data breaches, malware infections, and insider threats, and determining the appropriate level of protection needed to mitigate these risks effectively. Organizations may use risk assessment methodologies, such as qualitative or quantitative risk analysis, to evaluate and prioritize risks based on predefined criteria, such as severity, likelihood, and impact. Once risks have been identified and prioritized, organizations can then develop a security strategy and roadmap to guide their security program implementation efforts. This involves defining security goals and objectives, identifying key stakeholders and responsibilities, and establishing a timeline and budget for implementing security controls and practices. Organizations may use project management tools and techniques, such as Gantt charts or Agile methodologies, to plan and track their security program implementation efforts and ensure that milestones are met and resources are allocated effectively. One of the key components of a security program is establishing security policies and procedures to define the organization's security requirements and expectations and provide guidance on how to protect sensitive information and systems effectively. This includes developing policies and procedures for data classification and handling, access control, encryption, incident response, and security awareness training, among others. Organizations may use policy development frameworks, such as the NIST Cybersecurity Framework or ISO 27001, to guide their policy development efforts and ensure that policies are aligned with industry best practices and regulatory requirements. Once security policies and procedures have been developed, organizations must then implement security controls and practices to enforce these policies and protect their information assets and systems from potential threats and vulnerabilities. This may involve implementing technical controls, such as firewalls, antivirus software, intrusion detection and prevention systems (IDS/IPS), and encryption, to protect against external and internal threats and prevent unauthorized access to sensitive information and systems. Organizations may also implement administrative controls, such as security awareness training programs, access control policies, and incident response procedures, to educate employees about security risks and best practices and ensure compliance with security policies and regulations. In addition to implementing security controls and practices, organizations must also monitor and assess their security posture regularly to identify and address emerging threats and vulnerabilities proactively. This may involve conducting regular security assessments, vulnerability scans, penetration tests, and security audits to identify weaknesses and gaps in the organization's security defenses and prioritize remediation efforts accordingly. Organizations may use security information and event management (SIEM) solutions, intrusion detection and prevention systems (IDS/IPS), and security analytics tools to monitor and analyze security events and alerts and identify signs of suspicious or malicious activity. Finally, continuous improvement is essential for maintaining the effectiveness of a security program over time and adapting to evolving threats and technologies. This involves reviewing and updating security policies and procedures regularly to address emerging threats and vulnerabilities, incorporating lessons learned from security incidents and breaches, and staying informed about industry best practices and regulatory requirements. Organizations may use security metrics and key performance indicators (KPIs) to measure the effectiveness of their security program and identify areas for improvement, such as reducing incident response times, increasing employee security awareness, or improving patch management processes. By planning and implementing a comprehensive security program that addresses risk assessment, policy development, security controls and practices, monitoring and assessment, and continuous improvement, organizations can enhance their security posture and protect their sensitive data and systems from potential threats and vulnerabilities effectively.

Chapter 7: Basics of Information Security Management Systems (ISMS)

An Introduction to ISMS (Information Security Management System) provides a foundational understanding of the principles, components, and benefits of implementing an ISMS within an organization's cybersecurity framework. ISMS is a comprehensive approach to managing information security risks, encompassing policies, procedures, processes, and controls to protect sensitive data and systems from potential threats and vulnerabilities. One of the key components of an ISMS is the establishment of an information security policy that defines the organization's security objectives, goals, and responsibilities and provides guidance on how to protect sensitive information and systems effectively. Organizations may use ISO/IEC 27001, a globally recognized standard for information security management, as a framework for developing and implementing their ISMS. ISO/IEC 27001 provides a systematic approach to managing information security risks, including requirements for establishing an information security policy, conducting risk assessments, implementing security controls, and monitoring and reviewing the effectiveness of security measures. To implement an ISMS effectively, organizations must first conduct a comprehensive risk assessment to identify and prioritize security risks and vulnerabilities that could pose a threat to their information assets and systems. This involves assessing the likelihood and potential impact of various risks, such as data breaches, malware infections, and insider threats, and determining the appropriate level of protection needed to mitigate these risks effectively. Organizations may use risk assessment methodologies, such as qualitative or quantitative risk analysis, to evaluate and prioritize risks based on predefined criteria, such as severity, likelihood, and impact. Once risks have been identified and prioritized, organizations can then develop and implement security controls and practices to mitigate these risks effectively. This may involve implementing technical controls, such as firewalls, antivirus software, encryption, and intrusion detection and prevention systems (IDS/IPS), to protect against external and internal threats and prevent unauthorized access to sensitive information and systems. Organizations may also implement administrative controls, such as security awareness training programs, access control policies, and incident response procedures, to educate employees about security risks and best practices and ensure compliance with security policies and regulations. Implementing an ISMS also requires ongoing monitoring and review of the organization's security posture to identify and address emerging threats and vulnerabilities proactively. This may involve conducting regular security assessments, vulnerability scans, penetration tests, and security audits to identify weaknesses and gaps in the organization's security defenses and prioritize remediation efforts accordingly. Organizations may use security information and event management (SIEM) solutions, intrusion detection and prevention systems (IDS/IPS), and security analytics tools to monitor and analyze security events and alerts and identify signs of suspicious or malicious activity. Additionally, continuous improvement is essential for maintaining the effectiveness of an ISMS over time and adapting to evolving threats and technologies. This involves reviewing and updating security policies and procedures regularly to address emerging threats and vulnerabilities, incorporating lessons learned from security incidents and breaches, and staying informed about industry best practices and regulatory requirements. Organizations may use security metrics and key performance indicators (KPIs) to measure the effectiveness of their ISMS and identify areas for improvement, such as reducing incident response times, increasing employee security awareness, or improving patch management processes. By implementing an ISMS effectively, organizations can enhance their security posture and protect their sensitive data and systems from potential threats and vulnerabilities effectively. Components of an ISMS (Information Security Management System) encompass various elements crucial for establishing and maintaining effective information security practices within an organization's framework. One of the key components is the establishment of an information security policy that serves as the foundation for defining security objectives, responsibilities, and guidelines. To create an information security policy, organizations may use a text editor like Nano or Vim in a Linux environment or Notepad in Windows to draft a document outlining the organization's commitment to protecting sensitive information and systems. Another essential component is conducting risk assessments to identify and prioritize security risks and vulnerabilities that could jeopardize the organization's information assets and operations. Tools such as Nmap or OpenVAS can be used to scan networks and systems for potential vulnerabilities and assess their likelihood and impact. Following risk assessments, organizations must develop and implement security controls to mitigate identified risks effectively. This may involve configuring firewalls, antivirus software, and intrusion detection systems using commands such as iptables, ClamAV, and Snort, respectively, to protect against external threats and unauthorized access. Additionally, encryption techniques like OpenSSL can be employed to secure data both at rest and in transit, ensuring confidentiality and integrity. Access controls are another critical component of an ISMS, governing who can access sensitive information and systems and under what conditions. Access control lists (ACLs) can be configured using commands like chmod in Unix-based systems or cacls in Windows to specify user permissions and restrict unauthorized access to files and directories. Authentication mechanisms, such as passwords or biometrics, can be enforced using tools like passwd or useradd in Unix-based systems or net user in Windows to manage user accounts and credentials securely. Moreover, implementing security awareness training programs is essential to educate employees about security risks and best practices, fostering a culture of security awareness and accountability throughout the organization. Training sessions can be conducted using tools like PowerPoint or online learning platforms to cover topics such as phishing awareness, password hygiene, and incident reporting procedures. Incident response procedures are another critical component of an ISMS, providing a structured approach for detecting, responding to, and recovering from security incidents effectively.

Incident response plans can be developed using templates or frameworks like NIST SP 800-61 and should outline roles and responsibilities, escalation procedures, and communication protocols during a security incident. Additionally, organizations must establish monitoring and review processes to assess the effectiveness of their security controls continuously. Security information and event management (SIEM) solutions can be deployed to collect and analyze security logs and generate alerts for suspicious activity or anomalies. SIEM tools like Splunk or ELK Stack can help organizations correlate events from multiple sources and identify potential security incidents in real-time. Furthermore, organizations should conduct regular security audits and assessments to evaluate their compliance with internal policies, industry regulations, and best practices. Auditing tools like Lynis or Nessus can be used to scan systems for configuration errors, vulnerabilities, and compliance deviations and generate reports for remediation. Lastly, continuous improvement is crucial for maintaining the effectiveness of an ISMS over time. Organizations should review and update their security policies, procedures, and controls regularly to address emerging threats and evolving business requirements. Collaboration tools like Jira or Confluence can be used to track security improvement initiatives and prioritize enhancements based on risk assessments and feedback from security audits and incident response activities. By integrating these components effectively, organizations can establish a robust ISMS that protects their information assets and systems from potential threats and vulnerabilities while maintaining compliance with regulatory requirements and industry standards.

Chapter 8: Essentials of Information Security Policy Development

Developing security policies is a crucial aspect of establishing an effective information security management framework within an organization, providing clear guidelines and procedures for protecting sensitive data and systems from potential threats and vulnerabilities. One of the initial steps in developing security policies is conducting a thorough assessment of the organization's security requirements, risks, and compliance obligations to identify areas that require specific policies and controls. This assessment may involve reviewing relevant laws, regulations, and industry standards, such as GDPR, HIPAA, or PCI DSS, to ensure that policies align with legal and regulatory requirements. Once the security requirements have been identified, organizations can begin drafting security policies to address these needs effectively. Using a text editor like Nano or Vim in a Linux environment or Notepad in Windows, security policies can be written in a clear and concise manner, outlining the organization's expectations for security and defining the roles and responsibilities of employees, contractors, and third-party vendors. Security policies should cover various areas of information security, including data classification and handling, access control, encryption, incident response, and security awareness training, among others. When drafting security policies, it's essential to involve key stakeholders from across the organization, including IT, legal, human resources, and compliance departments, to ensure that policies are comprehensive, practical, and enforceable. Collaboration tools like Microsoft Teams or Slack can be used to facilitate communication and collaboration among stakeholders during the policy development process. Additionally, organizations should consider seeking input from employees and other relevant parties to gather feedback and address any concerns or questions they may have about the proposed policies. Once security policies have been drafted, they should undergo a thorough review and approval process to ensure accuracy, completeness, and compliance with internal standards and external regulations. This may involve circulating draft policies to stakeholders for review and feedback, incorporating any suggested revisions or amendments, and obtaining final approval from senior management or the organization's governing body. Version control systems like Git can be used to track changes to policies and document the review and approval process, ensuring that the final policies are up-to-date and properly authorized. After security policies have been approved, organizations must communicate them effectively to employees and other relevant parties to ensure awareness and compliance. This may involve distributing policies via email, posting them on the company intranet, or conducting training sessions to educate employees about their rights and responsibilities under the policies. Training materials can be created using tools like PowerPoint or online learning platforms to cover key topics, such as data protection, password hygiene, and incident reporting procedures. Additionally, organizations may consider implementing a policy acknowledgment process to ensure that employees have read and understood the policies and agree to comply with them. This may involve requiring employees to sign a statement acknowledging receipt of the policies and agreeing to abide by their terms and conditions. Electronic signature solutions like DocuSign or Adobe Sign can be used to collect and manage policy acknowledgments securely. Once security policies have been communicated and acknowledged, organizations must establish mechanisms for monitoring and enforcing compliance with the policies. This may involve conducting regular audits and assessments to evaluate adherence to policies and identify any areas of non-compliance or policy violations. Audit tools like Lynis or Nessus can be used to scan systems for configuration errors, vulnerabilities, and compliance deviations and generate reports for remediation. Additionally, organizations should establish procedures for reporting security incidents and breaches and investigate any suspected violations promptly and thoroughly. Incident response plans can be developed using templates or frameworks like NIST SP 800-61 and should outline roles and responsibilities, escalation procedures, and communication protocols during a security incident. By developing comprehensive security policies and ensuring effective communication, training, monitoring, and enforcement, organizations can establish a strong foundation for protecting their sensitive data and systems and maintaining compliance with legal, regulatory, and industry requirements.

Policy implementation and enforcement are critical components of an effective information security management framework, ensuring that security policies are effectively put into practice and adhered to throughout the organization. One of the first steps in implementing security policies is deploying technical controls to enforce policy requirements and mitigate security risks. This may involve configuring firewalls, intrusion detection systems (IDS), and antivirus software to monitor network traffic, detect suspicious activity, and prevent unauthorized access to sensitive data and systems. Commands such as iptables in Linux or netsh advfirewall in Windows can be used to configure firewall rules and filter network traffic based on predefined policies. Similarly, IDS/IPS solutions like Snort or Suricata can be deployed to analyze network packets and alert administrators to potential security threats or attacks. Additionally, antivirus software like ClamAV or Windows Defender can be installed on endpoints to detect and remove malware infections and protect against known threats. Alongside technical controls, organizations must establish administrative controls to enforce security policies and procedures effectively. This may involve creating user accounts with appropriate permissions and access levels using commands like useradd or usermod in Unix-based systems or net user in Windows. User accounts should be assigned roles and responsibilities based on the principle of least privilege, granting users access only to the resources and information necessary to perform their job duties. Access control lists (ACLs) can also be configured using commands like chmod in Unix-based systems or cacls in Windows to restrict access to files and directories and prevent unauthorized modifications or deletions. Furthermore, organizations should implement security awareness training programs to educate employees about security risks and best practices and ensure compliance with security policies and procedures. Training sessions can be conducted using tools like PowerPoint or online learning platforms to cover topics such as phishing awareness, password hygiene, and incident response procedures. Additionally, organizations may consider using phishing simulation tools like KnowBe4 or PhishMe to assess employee susceptibility to phishing attacks and reinforce training efforts. To enforce security policies effectively, organizations must establish procedures for monitoring and auditing compliance with policies and detecting and responding to policy violations. This may involve deploying security information and event management (SIEM) solutions to collect and analyze security logs and generate alerts for suspicious activity or policy violations. SIEM tools like Splunk or ELK Stack can help organizations correlate events from multiple sources and identify potential security incidents in real-time. Moreover, organizations should conduct regular security audits and assessments to evaluate compliance with internal policies, industry regulations, and best practices. Auditing tools like Lynis or Nessus can be used to scan systems for configuration errors, vulnerabilities, and compliance deviations and generate reports for remediation. Additionally, organizations must establish procedures for reporting security incidents and breaches and investigate any suspected violations promptly and thoroughly. Incident response plans can be developed using templates or frameworks like NIST SP 800-61 and should outline roles and responsibilities, escalation procedures, and communication protocols during a security incident. By implementing technical and administrative controls, providing security awareness training, and establishing procedures for monitoring and enforcing compliance, organizations can effectively implement and enforce security policies and reduce the risk of security breaches and data loss.

Chapter 9: Introduction to Information Security Standards and Frameworks

Common information security standards play a pivotal role in guiding organizations worldwide toward establishing robust frameworks for safeguarding their digital assets and mitigating risks effectively. One of the most widely adopted standards is ISO/IEC 27001, which provides a systematic approach to managing information security risks. Organizations seeking certification under ISO/IEC 27001 must adhere to its requirements, which include conducting risk assessments, implementing security controls, and establishing processes for continuous improvement. To implement ISO/IEC 27001 effectively, organizations typically start by identifying the scope of their information security management system (ISMS) and defining their security objectives and goals. This involves determining which assets are within the scope of the ISMS and documenting the organization's commitment to protecting sensitive information and systems. Once the scope and objectives have been defined, organizations must conduct a thorough risk assessment to identify and prioritize security risks and vulnerabilities that could impact their information assets and operations. This assessment may involve using tools like risk assessment software or spreadsheets to evaluate the likelihood and potential impact of various risks and determine the appropriate level of protection needed. Based on the results of the risk assessment, organizations must then implement security controls to mitigate identified risks effectively. ISO/IEC 27001 provides a comprehensive set of controls organized into 14 categories, including access control, cryptography, physical security, and incident management, among others. Organizations can use these controls as a basis for developing their security policies, procedures, and technical measures to address specific security risks and compliance requirements. For example, organizations may implement access control measures such as user authentication and authorization using commands like useradd or chmod in Unix-based systems or net user in Windows. They may also deploy encryption techniques like OpenSSL to protect sensitive data both at rest and in transit, ensuring confidentiality and integrity. Additionally, organizations may establish incident management processes and procedures to detect, respond to, and recover from security incidents effectively. This may involve developing incident response plans using frameworks like NIST SP 800-61 and establishing incident response teams with defined roles and responsibilities. Another common information security standard is the Payment Card Industry Data Security Standard (PCI DSS), which governs the protection of payment card data. Organizations that process, store, or transmit payment card data must comply with PCI DSS requirements to ensure the security of cardholder information and prevent data breaches. PCI DSS requirements cover various areas of information security, including network security, access control, encryption, and vulnerability management. To comply with PCI DSS, organizations must implement security controls such as firewalls, antivirus software, and intrusion detection systems to protect cardholder data and prevent unauthorized access. They must also encrypt cardholder data during transmission over public networks using secure protocols like TLS/SSL and ensure that cryptographic keys are managed securely. Additionally, organizations must conduct regular vulnerability scans and penetration tests to identify and remediate security vulnerabilities that could expose cardholder data to risk. Compliance with PCI DSS is validated through annual assessments conducted by qualified security assessors (QSAs) or through self-assessment questionnaires (SAQs) for smaller merchants and service providers. Another significant information security standard is the Health Insurance Portability and Accountability Act (HIPAA), which governs the protection of individually identifiable health information. Covered entities, such as healthcare providers, health plans, and healthcare clearinghouses, must comply with HIPAA requirements to ensure the privacy and security of protected health information (PHI). HIPAA requirements include implementing administrative, physical, and technical safeguards to protect PHI from unauthorized access, use, and disclosure. Administrative safeguards include policies, procedures, and training to ensure workforce compliance with HIPAA requirements, while physical safeguards involve measures to protect the physical security of facilities and equipment containing PHI. Technical safeguards encompass the use of access controls, encryption, and audit controls to protect electronic PHI (ePHI) stored or transmitted over data networks. To comply with HIPAA, covered entities must also conduct risk assessments to identify and mitigate security risks to ePHI and implement procedures for breach notification and response in the event of a security incident. Compliance with HIPAA is enforced by the Department of Health and Human Services (HHS), which may conduct audits and investigations to ensure that covered entities are adhering to HIPAA requirements. In summary, common information security standards such as ISO/IEC 27001, PCI DSS, and HIPAA provide organizations with frameworks for establishing robust information security management systems and protecting sensitive data and systems from potential threats and vulnerabilities. By complying with these standards and implementing appropriate security controls and measures, organizations can enhance their security posture and reduce the risk of security breaches and data loss. Frameworks for information security management serve as essential blueprints for organizations aiming to establish comprehensive strategies and protocols to safeguard their digital assets effectively. One of the most widely utilized frameworks is the NIST Cybersecurity Framework, developed by the National Institute of Standards and Technology, which provides a flexible approach for managing cybersecurity risks in critical infrastructure sectors. Organizations can leverage the NIST Cybersecurity Framework to assess their current cybersecurity posture, identify areas for improvement, and implement cybersecurity best practices to mitigate risks effectively. The framework consists of five core functions: Identify, Protect, Detect, Respond, and Recover, which organizations can tailor to their specific needs and risk profiles. To implement the NIST Cybersecurity Framework, organizations typically start by conducting a thorough assessment of their current cybersecurity posture using tools like vulnerability scanners or security assessment frameworks. This assessment helps organizations identify their critical assets, vulnerabilities, and potential threats, allowing them to prioritize their cybersecurity efforts and allocate resources effectively. Once the assessment is complete, organizations can begin implementing the core functions of the NIST Cybersecurity Framework. The "Identify" function involves identifying and documenting critical assets, systems, and data, as well as assessing risks to understand the organization's cybersecurity risk profile fully. This may involve using tools like asset management software or network scanners to catalog and categorize assets and identify potential vulnerabilities and exposures. The "Protect" function focuses on implementing safeguards to protect critical assets and systems from cybersecurity threats. This may include deploying firewalls, intrusion detection systems, and antivirus software to protect against external threats, as well as implementing access controls and encryption to safeguard sensitive data from unauthorized access or disclosure. Organizations may also develop security policies and procedures to govern the use of information systems and ensure compliance with security best practices. The "Detect" function involves implementing processes and tools to detect cybersecurity incidents promptly. This may include deploying security monitoring solutions such as security information and event management (SIEM) systems or intrusion detection systems (IDS) to monitor network traffic and detect signs of malicious activity or unauthorized access. Additionally, organizations may implement security controls such as log management and auditing to track and analyze security events and identify potential security incidents. The "Respond" function focuses on developing and implementing response procedures to address cybersecurity incidents effectively. This may include establishing an incident response team with defined roles and responsibilities and developing incident response plans to guide the organization's response to cybersecurity incidents. Incident response plans should outline steps for containing and mitigating the impact of security incidents, communicating with stakeholders, and restoring affected systems and data. The "Recover" function focuses on developing and implementing procedures to restore operations and services following a cybersecurity incident. This may include developing backup and recovery procedures to restore data and systems to a known good state, as well as implementing business continuity and disaster recovery plans to ensure the organization can continue operating during and after a cybersecurity incident. Additionally, organizations may conduct post-incident reviews to identify lessons learned and opportunities for improvement and update their cybersecurity policies and procedures accordingly. Another widely used framework for information security management is the ISO/IEC 27001 standard, which provides a systematic approach to managing information security risks. ISO/IEC 27001 is based on the Plan-Do-Check-Act (PDCA) model and consists of a series of requirements for establishing, implementing, maintaining, and continually improving an information security management system (ISMS). To implement ISO/IEC 27001 effectively, organizations typically start by conducting a gap analysis to assess their current information security practices against the requirements of the standard. This analysis helps organizations identify areas where they need to improve and develop an implementation plan to address any gaps. Once the implementation plan is in place, organizations can begin implementing the requirements of ISO/IEC 27001. This may involve developing and implementing policies, procedures, and controls to address the security requirements outlined in the standard. Organizations may also conduct training and awareness programs to educate employees about their roles and responsibilities under the ISMS and ensure compliance with security policies and procedures. Additionally, organizations may establish processes for monitoring and measuring the effectiveness of their ISMS and conducting internal audits to assess compliance with the standard. By leveraging frameworks such as the NIST Cybersecurity Framework and ISO/IEC 27001, organizations can establish comprehensive strategies and protocols for managing cybersecurity risks and protecting their digital assets effectively. These frameworks provide organizations with guidance and best practices for identifying, protecting, detecting, responding to, and recovering from cybersecurity incidents, helping them strengthen their cybersecurity posture and mitigate risks effectively.

Chapter 10: Best Practices for Security Awareness and Training

Security awareness strategies are crucial components of any organization's cybersecurity efforts, aiming to educate employees and stakeholders about potential security risks and best practices to mitigate them effectively. One effective strategy is to conduct regular security awareness training sessions for employees, covering topics such as phishing awareness, password hygiene, and social engineering tactics. These sessions can be conducted using various methods, including in-person training sessions, online courses, or interactive workshops, to accommodate different learning styles and preferences. Organizations may also leverage gamification techniques to make security training more engaging and interactive, such as creating quizzes, challenges, or simulations to reinforce key concepts and encourage participation. Additionally, organizations can use email newsletters, posters, and other communication channels to share security tips, updates, and reminders with employees regularly. These communications should be clear, concise, and easy to understand, focusing on practical steps employees can take to protect themselves and the organization from security threats. Another effective security awareness strategy is to establish a culture of security within the organization, where security is everyone's responsibility. This involves fostering a mindset of vigilance and accountability among employees, encouraging them to report suspicious activity or security incidents promptly and take proactive steps to protect sensitive information and systems. Organizations can promote a security-conscious culture by recognizing and rewarding employees who demonstrate good security practices, such as following security policies, reporting potential security threats, or completing security training modules. Additionally, organizations can appoint security champions or ambassadors within each department or team to serve as advocates for security awareness and help promote best practices among their colleagues. Furthermore, organizations can conduct simulated phishing exercises to test employees' awareness of phishing attacks and their ability to recognize and report suspicious emails. These exercises involve sending simulated phishing emails to employees and monitoring their responses to identify areas for improvement and provide targeted training and education where needed. Tools such as KnowBe4 or PhishMe can be used to create and manage simulated phishing campaigns and track employee engagement and performance over time. Moreover, organizations can leverage social engineering awareness training to educate employees about common social engineering tactics used by attackers to manipulate individuals into divulging sensitive information or performing actions that compromise security. This training may involve demonstrating how attackers use tactics such as pretexting, baiting, or tailgating to exploit human vulnerabilities and gain unauthorized access to systems or data. By raising awareness of these tactics and teaching employees how to recognize and respond to them effectively, organizations can reduce the risk of falling victim to social engineering attacks. Additionally, organizations can implement security awareness programs for remote workers to address the unique security challenges associated with remote work environments. These programs may include training on secure remote access methods, data protection best practices, and the use of virtual private networks (VPNs) and multi-factor authentication (MFA) to enhance security when working remotely. Furthermore, organizations can provide employees with resources and support to help them secure their home networks and devices, such as offering guidance on router configurations, software updates, and antivirus software installation. By empowering remote workers with the knowledge and tools they need to protect themselves and the organization from security threats, organizations can reduce the risk of security incidents and data breaches in remote work environments. In summary, security awareness strategies are essential for educating employees and stakeholders about cybersecurity risks and empowering them to take proactive steps to protect themselves and the organization from security threats. By conducting regular security awareness training sessions, promoting a culture of security, conducting simulated phishing exercises, and providing targeted education and support for remote workers, organizations can enhance their overall security posture and reduce the risk of security incidents and data breaches. Training methods and techniques are crucial components of any educational program or initiative, aiming to impart knowledge and skills to learners effectively. One commonly used training method is the lecture format, where an instructor delivers information to a group of learners verbally, typically using slides or visual aids to supplement the presentation. Lectures can be an effective way to convey large amounts of information efficiently, but they may not always be engaging or interactive, leading to reduced retention and learner engagement. To enhance the effectiveness of lectures, instructors can incorporate interactive elements such as quizzes, polls, or group discussions to encourage active participation and reinforce key concepts. Another popular training method is hands-on or experiential learning, where learners engage directly with the subject matter through practical exercises, simulations, or real-world scenarios. This approach allows learners to apply theoretical knowledge in a practical context, reinforcing learning and enhancing retention. Hands-on training can be particularly effective for teaching technical skills or procedures, such as software development, system administration, or troubleshooting techniques. Instructors can use virtual lab environments or simulation software to provide learners with realistic hands-on experiences without the need for expensive equipment or resources. Additionally, instructors can use case studies or role-playing exercises to simulate real-world scenarios and challenge learners to apply their knowledge and skills to solve practical problems. Another effective training technique is the flipped classroom model, where learners engage with instructional materials independently outside of class and then come together in class to discuss and apply what they have learned. In a flipped classroom, instructors typically provide learners with pre-recorded lectures, readings, or other instructional materials to review at their own pace before class. During class sessions, instructors can facilitate discussions, group activities, or problem-solving exercises to help learners deepen their understanding of the material and apply it to real-world situations. The flipped classroom model can promote active learning, critical thinking, and collaboration among learners, but it requires careful planning and preparation to ensure that learners engage with the materials outside of class and are prepared to participate in class discussions and activities. Another training technique is the use of multimedia and technology-based learning resources, such as videos, animations, interactive simulations, or online learning platforms. These resources can enhance the effectiveness of training by providing learners with engaging and interactive experiences that cater to different learning styles and preferences. For example, instructors can use video tutorials or screencasts to demonstrate complex concepts or procedures visually, making them easier for learners to understand and retain. Similarly, interactive simulations or gamified learning experiences can provide learners with opportunities to explore concepts in a hands-on and immersive way, promoting active engagement and knowledge retention. Additionally, online learning platforms or learning management systems (LMS) can provide learners with access to a wide range of educational resources, including videos, interactive modules, quizzes, and discussion forums, allowing them to learn at their own pace and on their own schedule. Instructors can use these platforms to deliver course materials, track learner progress, and facilitate communication and collaboration among learners. Moreover, collaborative learning techniques, such as group projects, peer review, or cooperative learning activities, can promote active engagement, critical thinking, and teamwork among learners. In a collaborative learning environment, learners work together to solve problems, complete tasks, or achieve shared goals, allowing them to leverage each other's strengths and perspectives to enhance their learning experience. Collaborative learning can be particularly effective for developing communication skills, interpersonal skills, and teamwork abilities, which are essential for success in many professional settings. Additionally, instructors can use assessment and feedback mechanisms to evaluate learner progress, identify areas for improvement, and provide learners with constructive feedback to support their learning goals. Assessment methods may include quizzes, exams, projects, or presentations, and feedback can be provided through written comments, rubrics, or one-on-one discussions. By incorporating a variety of training methods and techniques into their educational programs, instructors can create engaging, effective, and learner-centered learning experiences that cater to the diverse needs and preferences of their learners.

BOOK 2
MASTERING RISK MANAGEMENT IN INFORMATION SECURITY FOR CISM

ROB BOTWRIGHT

Chapter 1: Understanding Risk in Information Security

Risk identification methods are essential processes within any organization's risk management framework, crucial for identifying and assessing potential risks that may impact the achievement of its objectives or the success of its projects. One common method used for risk identification is brainstorming, where stakeholders from various departments or teams come together to generate ideas and identify potential risks associated with a particular project, process, or initiative. During a brainstorming session, participants can use techniques such as mind mapping or SWOT analysis to organize their thoughts and identify risks systematically. Additionally, organizations can conduct interviews or surveys with key stakeholders to gather insights and perspectives on potential risks and their potential impact on the organization. By engaging stakeholders directly in the risk identification process, organizations can leverage their expertise and experience to identify risks that may not be immediately apparent to others. Another effective method for identifying risks is document review, where organizations review existing documentation, such as project plans, process maps, or incident reports, to identify potential risks or issues that may have been documented previously. This may involve reviewing project documentation, such as project charters, scope statements, or risk registers, to identify risks that have been identified previously or to identify new risks that may have emerged since the project began. Organizations can also review incident reports or post-mortem analyses from previous projects or incidents to identify common themes or patterns and identify potential risks that may arise in similar situations in the future. Furthermore, organizations can conduct workshops or focus groups with subject matter experts (SMEs) to identify and assess potential risks associated with specific areas of the organization's operations, such as IT systems, supply chains, or regulatory compliance. These workshops or focus groups can provide a structured forum for discussing potential risks and their potential impact on the organization, allowing participants to share their knowledge and insights and identify risks collaboratively. Moreover, organizations can use risk assessment tools and techniques, such as risk matrices, risk heat maps, or risk scoring models, to systematically assess and prioritize potential risks based on their likelihood and impact. Risk matrices can help organizations visualize and prioritize risks based on their severity, allowing them to focus their resources and efforts on addressing the most significant risks first. Additionally, organizations can use risk heat maps to identify trends or patterns in the distribution of risks across different areas or departments, helping them allocate resources strategically to address areas of greatest concern. Another effective method for identifying risks is the use of checklists or templates, which provide a standardized framework for identifying and documenting potential risks associated with specific processes, activities, or projects. Organizations can develop checklists or templates based on industry best practices or regulatory requirements and use them to systematically identify and assess potential risks. By using checklists or templates, organizations can ensure that they consider all relevant factors and potential risks during the risk identification process and avoid overlooking important risks that may impact their objectives or operations. Additionally, organizations can leverage lessons learned from previous projects or incidents to identify and mitigate potential risks proactively. By analyzing past successes and failures and identifying common themes or root causes, organizations can identify potential risks that may arise in similar situations in the future and take steps to address them before they become significant issues. Moreover, organizations can use scenario analysis or "what-if" analysis to identify potential risks and their potential impact on the organization under different scenarios or conditions. This may involve simulating various scenarios or events and assessing their potential impact on the organization's objectives, operations, or stakeholders. By conducting scenario analysis, organizations can identify potential risks that may not be immediately apparent and develop contingency plans or risk mitigation strategies to address them proactively. Additionally, organizations can use data analysis techniques, such as trend analysis or predictive modeling, to identify potential risks based on historical data or trends. By analyzing data from various sources, such as sales figures, customer feedback, or operational metrics, organizations can identify patterns or anomalies that may indicate potential risks or issues that require further investigation. Data analysis techniques can help organizations identify potential risks early and take proactive measures to address them before they escalate into significant issues. In summary, risk identification methods are essential processes within any organization's risk management framework, crucial for identifying and assessing potential risks that may impact the achievement of its objectives or the success of its projects. By leveraging a variety of techniques and tools, such as brainstorming, document review, workshops, risk assessment tools, checklists, lessons learned, scenario analysis, and data analysis, organizations can systematically identify and assess potential risks and develop strategies to mitigate them effectively. Risk assessment tools are indispensable instruments within the arsenal of risk management, vital for systematically evaluating potential risks and vulnerabilities that may threaten the objectives or operations of an organization. One prevalent type of risk assessment tool is the risk matrix, which provides a visual representation of risks based on their likelihood and impact. Organizations typically categorize risks into levels based on predefined criteria, such as low, medium, or high likelihood, and low, medium, or high impact. This classification enables organizations to prioritize their risk mitigation efforts and allocate resources effectively. Additionally, risk matrices allow organizations to communicate risk information clearly and concisely to stakeholders, facilitating informed decision-making and risk management strategies. Another common risk assessment tool is the risk register, a centralized repository for capturing and managing information about identified risks. A risk register typically includes details such as the nature of the risk, its potential impact, likelihood, and severity, as well as mitigation measures and responsible parties. Organizations can use risk registers to track the status of identified risks, monitor changes over time, and ensure that appropriate actions are taken to address them effectively. Moreover, risk registers provide a valuable reference for risk management activities, such as risk monitoring, reporting, and decision-making, helping organizations maintain visibility and control over their risk landscape. Furthermore, organizations can use risk scoring models to assign numerical values to risks based on their likelihood and impact, enabling quantitative analysis and comparison of risks. Risk scoring models typically use predefined scales or algorithms to calculate risk scores, which organizations can use to prioritize risks and allocate resources based on their severity. By quantifying risks in this way, organizations can make more informed decisions about risk treatment options and resource allocation, maximizing the effectiveness of their risk management efforts. Additionally, organizations can use scenario analysis tools to simulate various scenarios or events and assess their potential impact on the organization's objectives or operations. Scenario analysis enables organizations to explore different risk scenarios and evaluate their consequences, helping them identify potential risks and develop contingency plans or risk mitigation strategies to address them proactively. Organizations can use scenario analysis tools to model a wide range of scenarios, such as natural disasters, cybersecurity incidents, or changes in market conditions, allowing them to anticipate and prepare for potential risks effectively. Moreover, organizations can use data analysis tools, such as trend analysis or predictive modeling, to identify potential risks based on historical data or trends. Trend analysis involves analyzing historical data to identify patterns, trends, or anomalies that may indicate potential risks or issues. By identifying patterns or trends in data, organizations can anticipate potential risks and take proactive measures to address them before they escalate into significant issues. Predictive modeling involves using statistical techniques or machine learning algorithms to analyze historical data and predict future outcomes or trends. By leveraging predictive modeling, organizations can forecast potential risks and develop strategies to mitigate them proactively, reducing the likelihood of adverse outcomes. Additionally, organizations can use risk assessment software or platforms to streamline the risk assessment process and manage risk information effectively. Risk assessment software typically provides features such as risk identification, assessment, analysis, and reporting, allowing organizations to standardize and automate their risk management activities. By using risk assessment software, organizations can centralize risk information, improve collaboration and communication among stakeholders, and ensure compliance with regulatory requirements and industry standards. Moreover, risk assessment software often includes built-in templates, frameworks, and libraries of best practices to help organizations get started quickly and effectively. By leveraging these resources, organizations can save time and effort and focus on addressing the most critical risks to their business. Additionally, organizations can use open-source risk assessment tools or frameworks to customize their risk management processes and adapt them to their specific needs and requirements. Open-source risk assessment tools typically provide flexibility, scalability, and customization options, allowing organizations to tailor their risk management activities to suit their unique circumstances. By using open-source risk assessment tools, organizations can benefit from community-driven development, ongoing support, and a wealth of resources and expertise from the open-source community. In summary, risk assessment tools are indispensable instruments within the arsenal of risk management, vital for systematically evaluating potential risks and vulnerabilities that may threaten the objectives or operations of an organization. By leveraging a variety of tools and techniques, such as risk matrices, risk registers, risk scoring models, scenario analysis, data analysis, risk assessment software, and open-source frameworks, organizations can identify, assess, and manage risks effectively, ensuring the resilience and success of their business endeavors.

Chapter 2: Risk Assessment Methodologies and Frameworks

Risk assessment methodologies provide structured approaches for identifying, evaluating, and managing risks within organizations, essential for informing decision-making and guiding risk management strategies effectively. One widely used risk assessment methodology is the Failure Mode and Effects Analysis (FMEA), which systematically analyzes potential failure modes within a system or process and their potential effects on system performance. FMEA involves identifying potential failure modes, assessing their severity, likelihood, and detectability, and prioritizing them based on their risk priority number (RPN). Organizations can use FMEA to identify critical failure modes and implement preventive or corrective actions to mitigate their impact effectively. Moreover, organizations can use the Hazard Analysis and Critical Control Points (HACCP) methodology to identify and mitigate potential hazards in food production and processing systems. HACCP involves identifying potential hazards, assessing their severity and likelihood, and implementing control measures to prevent, eliminate, or reduce the risk of foodborne illness or contamination. By following the principles of HACCP, organizations can ensure the safety and quality of their food products and comply with regulatory requirements and industry standards. Additionally, organizations can use the Bowtie Risk Assessment methodology to visualize and analyze complex risks and their potential consequences. Bowtie Risk Assessment involves identifying hazards, assessing their potential consequences, and implementing preventive and mitigative barriers to control the risk effectively. The bowtie diagram provides a visual representation of the risk scenario, with the hazard at the center, preventive barriers on one side, and mitigative barriers on the other side. Organizations can use the bowtie diagram to identify gaps in their risk management systems and develop strategies to strengthen their defenses against potential risks. Furthermore, organizations can use the Quantitative Risk Assessment (QRA) methodology to assess risks quantitatively and assign numerical values to risks based on their likelihood and impact. QRA involves gathering data, analyzing potential risks, and using mathematical models or statistical techniques to calculate risk scores or probabilities. By quantifying risks in this way, organizations can make more informed decisions about risk treatment options and allocate resources effectively. Additionally, organizations can use the ISO 31000 Risk Management standard as a framework for developing and implementing risk management processes and practices. ISO 31000 provides principles, guidelines, and a framework for managing risks systematically and effectively, helping organizations identify, assess, and treat risks consistently across their operations. By following the principles of ISO 31000, organizations can improve their risk management capabilities, enhance decision-making processes, and increase their resilience to potential risks. Moreover, organizations can use the COSO Enterprise Risk Management (ERM) framework to integrate risk management into their overall business strategy and operations. The COSO ERM framework provides a comprehensive approach to risk management, focusing on aligning risk management activities with organizational objectives and values. By following the COSO ERM framework, organizations can identify, assess, and manage risks in a systematic and integrated manner, helping them achieve their strategic goals and objectives more effectively. Additionally, organizations can use the Project Management Institute (PMI) Risk Management framework to manage risks within project environments effectively. The PMI Risk Management framework provides a structured approach for identifying, analyzing, and responding to risks throughout the project lifecycle, helping project managers anticipate and address potential issues before they escalate into significant problems. By following the PMI Risk Management framework, project managers can minimize the impact of risks on project outcomes and ensure the successful completion of their projects. Furthermore, organizations can use the National Institute of Standards and Technology (NIST) Cybersecurity Framework to assess and manage cybersecurity risks effectively. The NIST Cybersecurity Framework provides a flexible framework for managing cybersecurity risks, focusing on five core functions: identify, protect, detect, respond, and recover. By following the principles of the NIST Cybersecurity Framework, organizations can improve their cybersecurity posture, protect their critical assets, and enhance their resilience to cybersecurity threats. In summary, risk assessment methodologies provide structured approaches for identifying, evaluating, and managing risks within organizations, essential for informing decision-making and guiding risk management strategies effectively. By leveraging methodologies such as FMEA, HACCP, Bowtie Risk Assessment, QRA, ISO 31000, COSO ERM, PMI Risk Management, and the NIST Cybersecurity Framework, organizations can identify, assess, and manage risks systematically and effectively, ensuring the resilience and success of their business endeavors.

Comparing risk assessment frameworks is essential for organizations to select the most suitable approach for managing risks effectively in their specific context. One common comparison is between the ISO 27001 and NIST Cybersecurity Frameworks, both widely used in the field of cybersecurity. The ISO 27001 framework, based on the ISO/IEC 27001 standard, provides a systematic approach to managing information security risks. Organizations can use ISO 27001 to establish, implement, maintain, and continually improve an information security management system (ISMS). On the other hand, the NIST Cybersecurity Framework, developed by the National Institute of Standards and Technology (NIST) in the United States, offers a flexible framework for managing cybersecurity risks. While ISO 27001 focuses specifically on information security, the NIST Cybersecurity Framework provides a broader, risk-based approach to cybersecurity that encompasses people, processes, and technology. Another comparison is between the COSO Enterprise Risk Management (ERM) framework and the ISO 31000 Risk Management standard. Both frameworks provide principles, guidelines, and a framework for managing risks systematically and effectively. The COSO ERM framework, developed by the Committee of Sponsoring Organizations of the Treadway Commission (COSO), focuses on integrating risk management into an organization's overall business strategy and operations. In contrast, the ISO 31000 standard provides a more general framework for managing risks across different disciplines and sectors. While the COSO ERM framework emphasizes aligning risk management with organizational objectives and values, ISO 31000 offers a more flexible and scalable approach that can be tailored to the specific needs and context of an organization. Moreover, organizations may compare risk assessment frameworks based on their industry or regulatory requirements. For example, organizations operating in the healthcare sector may compare the HIPAA Security Rule and the NIST Cybersecurity Framework for managing cybersecurity risks. The HIPAA Security Rule, developed by the U.S. Department of Health and Human Services (HHS), sets standards for protecting electronic protected health information (ePHI). Organizations subject to HIPAA regulations must comply with the Security Rule's requirements for safeguarding ePHI. In contrast, the NIST Cybersecurity Framework provides a risk-based approach to cybersecurity that can complement and enhance an organization's compliance efforts with HIPAA regulations. Similarly, organizations in the financial services industry may compare the Basel III framework and the ISO 31000 standard for managing financial risks.

Basel III, developed by the Basel Committee on Banking Supervision, sets capital requirements and risk management standards for banks and financial institutions. In contrast, the ISO 31000 standard offers a more general framework for managing risks across different sectors and disciplines, including finance. Organizations may compare these frameworks to identify areas of overlap or complementarity and develop integrated risk management strategies that address both regulatory requirements and broader organizational objectives. Furthermore, organizations may consider the maturity and scalability of risk assessment frameworks when comparing them. Some frameworks may be more suitable for organizations with mature risk management practices and sophisticated risk management capabilities, while others may be better suited for organizations that are just beginning their risk management journey or operating in dynamic and rapidly changing environments. Additionally, organizations may consider the level of guidance and support provided by each framework, such as training materials, implementation guides, and certification programs. Frameworks that offer comprehensive resources and support can help organizations implement risk management practices more effectively and achieve better outcomes. Ultimately, the choice of a risk assessment framework depends on various factors, including the organization's industry, regulatory requirements, risk management maturity, and specific needs and objectives. By comparing different frameworks based on these factors, organizations can select the most suitable approach for managing risks effectively and achieving their strategic goals.

Chapter 3: Quantitative Risk Analysis Techniques

Probability and impact analysis is a fundamental technique used in risk management to assess the likelihood and consequences of potential risks on project objectives, operations, or outcomes. In probability and impact analysis, risks are evaluated based on two key factors: their probability of occurrence and the impact they would have if they were to materialize. To conduct a probability and impact analysis, organizations typically use a qualitative or quantitative approach, depending on the nature of the risks and the available data. In a qualitative probability and impact analysis, risks are assessed subjectively based on expert judgment, experience, and knowledge of the organization and its environment. Organizations may use risk matrices or scoring models to categorize risks into levels based on their likelihood and impact. For example, risks may be categorized as low, medium, or high likelihood and low, medium, or high impact, allowing organizations to prioritize their risk mitigation efforts accordingly. Moreover, organizations can use scenario analysis or "what-if" analysis to assess the potential impact of different risk scenarios on project objectives or outcomes. By simulating various scenarios or events and evaluating their consequences, organizations can identify potential risks and develop strategies to mitigate them proactively. In contrast, quantitative probability and impact analysis involves using statistical techniques or mathematical models to assess risks objectively based on data and empirical evidence. Organizations may use historical data, probability distributions, or Monte Carlo simulations to calculate the likelihood of risks occurring and their potential impact on project objectives or outcomes. For example, organizations may use historical data on project delays or cost overruns to estimate the probability of similar risks occurring in future projects and their potential impact on project schedules or budgets. Additionally, organizations can use sensitivity analysis or scenario modeling to assess the sensitivity of project outcomes to changes in key risk factors. By varying input parameters or assumptions and evaluating their impact on project outcomes, organizations can identify the most significant risks and develop strategies to mitigate their effects effectively. Furthermore, organizations can use risk assessment tools and software to streamline the probability and impact analysis process and manage risk information more effectively. Risk assessment tools typically provide features such as risk identification, assessment, analysis, and reporting, allowing organizations to standardize and automate their risk management activities. By using risk assessment tools, organizations can facilitate collaboration among stakeholders, improve decision-making processes, and ensure compliance with regulatory requirements and industry standards. Additionally, organizations can use historical data or lessons learned from previous projects to inform their probability and impact analysis. By analyzing past successes and failures and identifying common themes or patterns, organizations can anticipate potential risks and develop strategies to mitigate them proactively. For example, organizations may use historical data on project delays or cost overruns to identify common causes or root causes and implement preventive measures to address them in future projects. Moreover, organizations can use risk registers or risk databases to capture and track information about identified risks and their potential impact on project objectives or outcomes. Risk registers typically include details such as the nature of the risk, its potential consequences, likelihood, severity, and mitigation measures, allowing organizations to monitor changes over time and ensure that appropriate actions are taken to address risks effectively. Additionally, organizations can use risk scoring models or risk prioritization techniques to rank risks based on their likelihood and impact and prioritize them for further analysis or mitigation. By focusing their efforts on addressing the most significant risks first, organizations can allocate resources effectively and maximize the effectiveness of their risk management efforts. In summary, probability and impact analysis is a fundamental technique used in risk management to assess the likelihood and consequences of potential risks on project objectives, operations, or outcomes. By conducting qualitative or quantitative probability and impact analysis, leveraging historical data or lessons learned, using risk assessment tools and software, and prioritizing risks effectively, organizations can identify, assess, and mitigate risks proactively, ensuring the success and resilience of their projects and operations.

Cost-benefit analysis is a critical tool in risk management, providing a systematic approach to evaluating the potential costs and benefits of risk mitigation strategies and informing decision-making processes. In cost-benefit analysis, organizations compare the expected costs of implementing risk mitigation measures against the anticipated benefits in terms of risk reduction or avoidance. One common method used in cost-benefit analysis is the net present value (NPV) approach, which calculates the present value of future costs and benefits to determine whether a risk mitigation strategy is financially viable. To perform a cost-benefit analysis using the NPV approach, organizations first estimate the costs associated with implementing risk mitigation measures, including expenses such as equipment, personnel, training, and ongoing maintenance. Once the costs have been identified, organizations estimate the expected benefits of implementing the risk mitigation measures, such as reduced losses, improved operational efficiency, increased revenue, or enhanced reputation. By comparing the present value of the expected benefits against the present value of the costs, organizations can determine whether the risk mitigation strategy is economically justified. Moreover, organizations may use sensitivity analysis to assess the impact of uncertainty or variability on the results of the cost-benefit analysis. Sensitivity analysis involves varying key input parameters or assumptions within a range of values and evaluating their effect on the outcomes of the analysis. By identifying the most sensitive variables or factors, organizations can focus their attention on managing or reducing uncertainty and improving the robustness of the cost-benefit analysis. Additionally, organizations can use decision trees to model different scenarios and evaluate the potential outcomes of alternative risk mitigation strategies. Decision trees provide a graphical representation of decision-making processes, including various decision options, possible outcomes, and their associated probabilities and costs. By analyzing different branches of the decision tree and calculating the expected value of each option, organizations can identify the most favorable course of action and make informed decisions about risk management strategies. Furthermore, organizations may consider qualitative factors, such as reputational risk, regulatory compliance, or strategic alignment, when conducting cost-benefit analysis. While quantitative analysis focuses on tangible costs and benefits, qualitative analysis considers intangible factors that may influence decision-making and risk management outcomes. By incorporating qualitative factors into the cost-benefit analysis, organizations can ensure a more comprehensive and holistic assessment of the potential impacts of risk mitigation strategies. Moreover, organizations can use cost-effectiveness analysis to compare the relative efficiency of different risk mitigation measures in achieving a specific objective. Cost-effectiveness analysis involves calculating the cost per unit of a desired outcome, such as the cost per unit of risk reduction or the cost per unit of avoided loss. By comparing the cost-effectiveness of alternative risk mitigation measures, organizations can identify the most efficient use of resources and maximize the value of their risk management investments. Additionally, organizations can use cost-benefit analysis to prioritize risk mitigation efforts and allocate resources effectively. By comparing the expected costs and benefits of different risk mitigation measures, organizations can identify the most cost-effective options and focus their resources on addressing the most significant risks first. Moreover, organizations can use cost-benefit analysis to communicate the rationale for risk management decisions and garner support from stakeholders. By presenting the results of the analysis in a clear and compelling manner, organizations can demonstrate the value of investing in risk mitigation measures and justify their decisions to key stakeholders, such as executives, board members, regulators, and shareholders. In summary, cost-benefit analysis is a critical tool in risk management, providing a systematic approach to evaluating the potential costs and benefits of risk mitigation strategies and informing decision-making processes. By using techniques such as the net present value approach, sensitivity analysis, decision trees, qualitative analysis, and cost-effectiveness analysis, organizations can assess the economic viability, efficiency, and effectiveness of risk management strategies and make informed decisions about allocating resources and managing risks effectively.

Chapter 4: Qualitative Risk Analysis Approaches

Risk ranking and scoring methods are essential techniques used in risk management to prioritize risks based on their likelihood, impact, and other relevant factors, enabling organizations to focus their resources on addressing the most significant risks first. One common method for ranking and scoring risks is the risk matrix, which categorizes risks into different levels based on their likelihood and impact. To create a risk matrix, organizations typically define a set of criteria for assessing the likelihood and impact of risks and assign scores or ratings to each criterion. For example, organizations may use a scale of 1 to 5 to assess the likelihood and impact of risks, with 1 representing low likelihood or impact and 5 representing high likelihood or impact. Once the criteria and scoring system have been established, organizations can plot the likelihood and impact scores of each risk on a matrix or grid, with the likelihood scores on one axis and the impact scores on the other axis. By mapping the likelihood and impact scores of each risk on the risk matrix, organizations can categorize risks into different levels, such as low, medium, or high risk, based on predefined thresholds or boundaries. Another method for ranking and scoring risks is the risk scoring model, which assigns numerical scores or weights to different risk factors and calculates an overall risk score for each risk. To develop a risk scoring model, organizations first identify and define the risk factors or criteria that are relevant to assessing the likelihood and impact of risks in their specific context. For example, organizations may consider factors such as the probability of occurrence, the severity of consequences, the level of exposure, and the effectiveness of existing controls when scoring risks. Once the risk factors have been identified, organizations assign numerical scores or weights to each factor based on their relative importance or significance in determining the overall risk level. Organizations may use a variety of techniques to assign scores or weights to risk factors, such as expert judgment, historical data analysis, or statistical methods. Once the scores or weights have been assigned to the risk factors, organizations calculate an overall risk score for each risk by aggregating the scores of individual factors. The overall risk score provides a quantitative measure of the risk level, allowing organizations to prioritize risks based on their relative severity or significance. Moreover, organizations can use risk ranking and scoring methods to compare risks across different projects, departments, or business units and identify common themes or patterns that may require attention. By aggregating and analyzing risk data from multiple sources, organizations can gain insights into the overall risk profile of the organization and make informed decisions about resource allocation and risk management priorities. Furthermore, organizations may use risk ranking and scoring methods to support decision-making processes, such as project selection, investment prioritization, or risk treatment planning. By providing a systematic and transparent way to assess and prioritize risks, risk ranking and scoring methods help ensure that resources are allocated effectively and risk management efforts are focused on addressing the most significant risks first. Additionally, organizations can use risk ranking and scoring methods to communicate risk information to stakeholders and facilitate discussions about risk management priorities and strategies. By presenting risk data in a clear and structured manner, organizations can help stakeholders understand the relative importance of different risks and make informed decisions about risk management actions. In summary, risk ranking and scoring methods are essential techniques used in risk management to prioritize risks based on their likelihood, impact, and other relevant factors. By using methods such as the risk matrix and risk scoring model, organizations can categorize risks, assign numerical scores, and calculate overall risk scores, enabling them to focus their resources on addressing the most significant risks first and making informed decisions about risk management priorities and strategies. Expert judgment plays a crucial role in qualitative risk analysis, providing valuable insights and expertise to assess risks based on subjective judgment, experience, and knowledge. In qualitative risk analysis, expert judgment involves gathering input and opinions from individuals with relevant experience and expertise in the subject matter to evaluate risks and their potential impacts. One common method for leveraging expert judgment in qualitative risk analysis is the Delphi technique, which involves soliciting input from a panel of experts through a series of structured questionnaires or surveys. To deploy the Delphi technique, organizations first select a panel of experts representing diverse perspectives and areas of expertise relevant to the risks being assessed. The experts are then asked to independently evaluate and rank the identified risks based on their likelihood, impact, and other relevant factors using a standardized questionnaire or survey. After completing the initial round of assessments, the responses are compiled and summarized, and the experts are provided with feedback on their assessments, including the range of responses and any areas of disagreement or consensus. The experts are then asked to reconsider their assessments in light of the feedback and submit revised responses in a subsequent round of evaluations. This iterative process continues until a consensus is reached among the experts, typically defined as a predetermined level of agreement or convergence in their assessments. Another method for leveraging expert judgment in qualitative risk analysis is the brainstorming technique, which involves gathering a group of experts together to generate ideas, identify risks, and evaluate their potential impacts collaboratively. To deploy the brainstorming technique, organizations convene a group of experts representing diverse perspectives and areas of expertise relevant to the risks being assessed. The group is then facilitated through a structured brainstorming session, during which participants are encouraged to generate ideas and identify risks associated with the project, process, or activity under consideration. As risks are identified, the group evaluates each risk based on its likelihood, impact, and other relevant factors, using their collective expertise and judgment to assess the potential consequences and prioritize risks for further analysis or action. Moreover, organizations may use structured workshops or focus groups to leverage expert judgment in qualitative risk analysis. Structured workshops involve bringing together a group of experts for a facilitated discussion or series of discussions focused on assessing risks and their potential impacts. The facilitator guides the group through a structured agenda, ensuring that key topics are addressed, and encouraging active participation and collaboration among participants. Similarly, focus groups involve convening a small group of experts to discuss specific topics or issues related to risk assessment and management. By providing a forum for open discussion and debate, structured workshops and focus groups enable organizations to leverage the collective knowledge, experience, and insights of experts to assess risks comprehensively and make informed decisions about risk management strategies. Furthermore, organizations may use expert judgment to validate and refine the results of quantitative risk analysis techniques, such as Monte Carlo simulations or probabilistic risk models. Quantitative risk analysis involves using mathematical models and statistical techniques to assess risks objectively based on data and empirical evidence. However, quantitative risk analysis may be limited by data availability, uncertainty, and complexity, making it challenging to obtain precise estimates of risk likelihood and impact. In such cases, organizations may supplement quantitative analysis with expert judgment to validate the results, identify areas of uncertainty or disagreement, and refine the risk assessments accordingly. Additionally, organizations may use expert judgment to assess risks that are difficult to quantify or predict, such as emerging risks, strategic risks, or reputational risks. While quantitative risk analysis techniques are valuable for assessing risks with well-defined probabilities and consequences, they may be less effective for evaluating risks with uncertain or qualitative attributes. In such cases, organizations rely on expert judgment to provide qualitative insights and subjective assessments based on experience, intuition, and professional judgment. In summary, expert judgment is a valuable and essential tool in qualitative risk analysis, providing organizations with valuable insights and expertise to assess risks comprehensively and make informed decisions about risk management strategies. By leveraging techniques such as the Delphi technique, brainstorming, structured workshops, and focus groups, organizations can harness the collective knowledge and experience of experts to identify, evaluate, and prioritize risks effectively, ensuring the success and resilience of their projects, processes, and operations.

Chapter 5: Risk Treatment Strategies and Mitigation Measures

Risk mitigation planning is an integral component of risk management strategies, crucial for safeguarding organizations against potential threats and vulnerabilities that could adversely affect their operations, projects, or objectives. When initiating the risk mitigation planning process, organizations typically commence by identifying and prioritizing risks through various methodologies such as risk assessments, workshops, or data analysis. By employing techniques like risk registers or risk matrices, organizations compile a comprehensive list of potential risks, categorizing them based on their likelihood and impact. Once risks have been identified and prioritized, the next step involves developing tailored risk mitigation plans to address each identified risk effectively. This process entails assessing the potential consequences of each risk and formulating strategies to either reduce the likelihood of occurrence or minimize its impact should it materialize.

In practical terms, organizations may utilize risk mitigation strategies such as risk avoidance, risk transfer, risk reduction, or risk acceptance, depending on the nature and severity of the identified risks. For instance, if a particular risk poses a significant threat to the project's success, organizations may opt for risk avoidance by altering project scope or objectives to circumvent the risk altogether. Conversely, organizations may choose risk transfer by outsourcing certain activities or purchasing insurance to mitigate the financial impact of potential risks. Moreover, risk reduction strategies involve implementing preventive measures or controls to mitigate the likelihood or severity of identified risks. This could entail enhancing cybersecurity measures, implementing backup systems, or conducting regular maintenance to mitigate the risk of system failures or data breaches.

To facilitate the risk mitigation planning process, organizations often establish risk management teams comprising stakeholders with diverse expertise and perspectives. These teams collaborate to assess risks comprehensively, leveraging their collective knowledge to identify effective mitigation strategies. Furthermore, risk mitigation plans are dynamic documents that require regular review and updates to remain relevant and effective in the face of evolving threats and changing organizational circumstances. Therefore, organizations incorporate mechanisms for ongoing monitoring and evaluation of risk mitigation measures to ensure their continued efficacy.

In addition to internal risk management processes, organizations may also collaborate with external partners, consultants, or industry peers to gain insights into emerging risks and best practices in risk mitigation. By participating in industry forums, conferences, or information-sharing networks, organizations can stay abreast of evolving threats and leverage collective intelligence to enhance their risk mitigation strategies.

Furthermore, technology plays a crucial role in facilitating risk mitigation planning and implementation. Risk management software solutions offer features such as risk registers, workflow automation, and reporting capabilities, streamlining the entire risk mitigation process. These tools enable organizations to centralize risk-related data, track mitigation activities, and generate real-time reports to inform decision-making. For instance, organizations may utilize project management platforms like Jira or Trello to track and manage risk mitigation tasks, assigning responsibilities and monitoring progress effectively.

Moreover, organizations may deploy specialized software solutions such as risk assessment tools or cybersecurity platforms to assess and mitigate specific types of risks comprehensively. For instance, vulnerability scanning tools like Nessus or Qualys can help organizations identify and address security vulnerabilities in their IT infrastructure, while compliance management platforms like ServiceNow or ZenGRC assist in ensuring adherence to regulatory requirements and industry standards.

Additionally, organizations may conduct scenario-based simulations or tabletop exercises to test the effectiveness of their risk mitigation plans and enhance preparedness for potential crises or emergencies. By simulating various risk scenarios, organizations can evaluate the responsiveness of their teams, identify gaps in existing mitigation measures, and refine their response strategies accordingly.

Overall, risk mitigation planning is a proactive and iterative process aimed at minimizing the impact of potential risks on organizational objectives. Through a combination of strategic planning, collaboration, and leveraging technology, organizations can develop robust risk mitigation plans that enhance resilience and safeguard their operations against unforeseen threats and vulnerabilities.

Control implementation and monitoring are fundamental processes within the realm of risk management, essential for ensuring the effectiveness and efficiency of control measures deployed to mitigate identified risks. When initiating control implementation, organizations typically begin by translating their risk mitigation plans into actionable control strategies tailored to address specific risks identified during the risk assessment phase. This involves selecting appropriate controls from a range of options available, such as technical controls, administrative controls, or physical controls, depending on the nature of the risks and the organization's risk appetite. For example, in the context of cybersecurity, organizations may implement technical controls like firewalls, antivirus software, or intrusion detection systems to protect against cyber threats, while administrative controls such as policies, procedures, and training programs help establish security protocols and promote employee awareness.

To deploy control measures effectively, organizations often utilize project management methodologies and tools to plan, execute, and monitor control implementation activities systematically. For instance, organizations may adopt frameworks like the Project Management Body of Knowledge (PMBOK) or Agile methodologies to manage control implementation projects, breaking down tasks into manageable units, assigning responsibilities, and tracking progress using project management software like Microsoft Project or Asana. By establishing clear timelines, milestones, and deliverables, organizations can ensure that control implementation activities proceed according to plan and are completed within predefined budgets and resource constraints.

Moreover, control implementation often requires collaboration across different departments or functional areas within the organization to ensure alignment with overall business objectives and regulatory requirements. For example, in large organizations, control implementation projects may involve cross-functional teams comprising representatives from IT, legal, compliance, finance, and operations, each contributing their expertise to ensure the successful deployment of control measures. By fostering collaboration and communication among stakeholders, organizations can streamline the implementation process, resolve conflicts, and address any obstacles or challenges that may arise during the execution of control initiatives.

Furthermore, organizations may leverage automation and technology to streamline control implementation processes and enhance efficiency. For example, organizations can use configuration management tools like Ansible or Puppet to automate the deployment and configuration of IT controls, ensuring consistency and standardization across systems and environments. Similarly, organizations may utilize continuous monitoring solutions like Nagios or Prometheus to monitor the effectiveness of control measures in real-time, detecting and responding to security incidents or deviations from established baselines promptly.

Once control measures have been implemented, organizations must establish mechanisms for ongoing monitoring and evaluation to ensure their continued effectiveness and relevance in mitigating identified risks. This involves establishing key performance indicators (KPIs) and metrics to measure the performance and impact of control measures over time. For example, organizations may track metrics such as the number of security incidents detected, the response time to incidents, or the percentage of compliance with established control objectives to assess the effectiveness of control measures.

Moreover, organizations may conduct periodic reviews and audits of control implementation projects to assess adherence to project plans, identify areas for improvement, and address any gaps or deficiencies in control measures. For example, organizations may conduct internal audits or third-party assessments to evaluate the effectiveness of control measures in mitigating risks and ensuring compliance with regulatory requirements and industry standards. By conducting regular reviews and audits, organizations can identify emerging risks, adapt control measures to evolving threats, and continuously improve their risk management practices.

Additionally, organizations may establish governance structures and committees responsible for overseeing control implementation and monitoring activities, ensuring accountability and oversight at the highest levels of the organization. For example, organizations may establish risk management committees or steering committees comprising senior executives and key stakeholders to provide strategic direction, guidance, and support for control implementation initiatives. By involving senior leadership in the oversight of control implementation projects, organizations can demonstrate commitment to risk management objectives and ensure alignment with overall business strategies.

In summary, control implementation and monitoring are critical components of effective risk management practices, essential for mitigating identified risks and safeguarding organizational assets and resources. By deploying control measures systematically, leveraging project management methodologies and technology, and establishing mechanisms for ongoing monitoring and evaluation, organizations can enhance resilience, ensure compliance with regulatory requirements, and protect against emerging threats and vulnerabilities.

Chapter 6: Implementing Risk Management Processes in Organizations

Establishing risk management frameworks is a crucial endeavor for organizations seeking to effectively identify, assess, mitigate, and monitor risks across their operations, projects, and strategic initiatives. One commonly employed framework for risk management is the ISO 31000 standard, which provides guidelines and principles for implementing risk management processes systematically. To adopt the ISO 31000 framework, organizations typically begin by conducting a risk assessment to identify and prioritize risks relevant to their objectives and context. This involves leveraging techniques such as risk registers, risk matrices, or risk workshops to systematically catalog potential threats, vulnerabilities, and opportunities that may impact organizational performance or objectives. Once risks have been identified, organizations assess their likelihood and potential impact, using qualitative or quantitative analysis methodologies to prioritize risks based on their severity and significance.

To facilitate the risk assessment process, organizations may utilize risk assessment software tools like RiskLens or RiskWatch, which provide features such as risk scoring, scenario analysis, and reporting capabilities to streamline data collection, analysis, and visualization. Additionally, organizations may leverage industry-specific frameworks or standards to supplement their risk management efforts and address sector-specific challenges and requirements. For example, organizations operating in the financial services sector may adopt frameworks such as the Basel II or III frameworks to manage credit, market, and operational risks effectively.

Moreover, organizations may establish risk management committees or working groups comprising representatives from different functional areas to oversee the development and implementation of risk management frameworks. These committees provide governance and oversight, ensuring that risk management processes align with organizational objectives, policies, and regulatory requirements. Furthermore, organizations may establish risk appetite statements or risk tolerance thresholds to define acceptable levels of risk exposure and guide decision-making regarding risk management strategies.

In addition to identifying and assessing risks, organizations must develop risk treatment plans to mitigate or manage identified risks effectively. This involves selecting and implementing appropriate risk mitigation strategies, such as risk avoidance, risk reduction, risk transfer, or risk acceptance, based on the organization's risk appetite and objectives. For example, organizations may choose to mitigate cybersecurity risks by implementing technical controls like firewalls, intrusion detection systems, or encryption protocols to protect sensitive data and systems from unauthorized access or cyber attacks.

Furthermore, organizations may conduct regular risk monitoring and reviews to track changes in risk exposure, assess the effectiveness of risk mitigation measures, and identify emerging risks or trends that may impact organizational objectives. This involves establishing key performance indicators (KPIs) and risk metrics to measure and monitor risk-related performance over time. For example, organizations may track metrics such as the number of security incidents detected, the response time to incidents, or the level of compliance with established risk management processes to assess the effectiveness of risk mitigation efforts.

Additionally, organizations may leverage risk management software tools like RSA Archer or MetricStream to automate and streamline risk monitoring activities, providing real-time insights into risk exposure and enabling proactive risk management responses. By integrating risk management processes with other organizational systems and processes, such as enterprise resource planning (ERP) systems or business intelligence platforms, organizations can enhance visibility and decision-making capabilities regarding risk-related issues.

Moreover, organizations may conduct periodic risk assessments or audits to evaluate the effectiveness of risk management frameworks and identify opportunities for improvement. This involves reviewing risk management policies, procedures, and controls to ensure alignment with organizational objectives, regulatory requirements, and industry best practices. Additionally, organizations may conduct scenario-based risk assessments or stress tests to simulate potential risk scenarios and evaluate the resilience of risk management frameworks under adverse conditions.

Furthermore, organizations may establish incident response and crisis management plans to address unforeseen events or emergencies that may impact organizational objectives or operations. This involves defining roles, responsibilities, and communication protocols for responding to incidents effectively and minimizing their impact on business continuity and reputation. By integrating incident response plans with risk management frameworks, organizations can ensure a coordinated and effective response to incidents, enabling them to mitigate risks and recover from disruptions efficiently.

In summary, establishing risk management frameworks is essential for organizations to proactively identify, assess, mitigate, and monitor risks across their operations and strategic initiatives. By adopting internationally recognized standards and frameworks, leveraging technology-enabled solutions, and fostering a culture of risk awareness and accountability, organizations can enhance resilience, optimize decision-making, and achieve their objectives in an uncertain and dynamic business environment. Integrating risk management into business processes is imperative for organizations aiming to foster a culture of risk-awareness and resilience across all levels of their operations and decision-making. One effective approach to achieving this integration is by embedding risk management practices directly into existing business processes and workflows, thereby ensuring that risk considerations are systematically addressed throughout the organization's activities. To initiate this integration process, organizations often conduct a comprehensive review of their existing business processes to identify potential areas of risk exposure or vulnerability. This involves mapping out key processes, workflows, and decision points to understand how risks may manifest and impact organizational objectives or outcomes.

Once potential risk areas have been identified, organizations can implement risk management controls and measures directly within these processes to mitigate or manage the identified risks effectively. This may involve incorporating risk assessment checkpoints, control mechanisms, or decision gates into existing workflows to ensure that risk considerations are systematically evaluated and addressed at each stage of the process. For example, organizations may introduce risk assessment templates or questionnaires to be completed by process owners or stakeholders before proceeding with critical activities or decisions.

Furthermore, organizations may leverage technology-enabled solutions to facilitate the integration of risk management into business processes. For instance, organizations may deploy enterprise risk management (ERM) software platforms like Riskonnect or LogicManager, which provide features such as risk assessment tools, workflow automation, and reporting capabilities to streamline risk management processes and embed risk considerations directly into existing workflows. By utilizing these platforms, organizations can centralize risk-related data, track risk assessments and controls, and generate real-time reports to inform decision-making and risk prioritization.

Additionally, organizations may establish risk management roles and responsibilities within existing process teams or committees to ensure that risk considerations are adequately addressed and escalated as needed. This may involve appointing risk champions or coordinators within each business unit or functional area to oversee risk management activities, coordinate risk assessments, and liaise with central risk management functions. By embedding risk management expertise directly within process teams, organizations can ensure that risk considerations are integrated seamlessly into day-to-day operations and decision-making processes.

Moreover, organizations may conduct training and awareness programs to educate employees and stakeholders about the importance of risk management and their roles and responsibilities in identifying, assessing, and managing risks within their respective areas of operation. This may involve providing training sessions, workshops, or online modules to familiarize employees with risk management concepts, tools, and techniques and empower them to proactively identify and address risks in their daily work activities.

Furthermore, organizations may establish performance metrics and key performance indicators (KPIs) to measure the effectiveness of risk management integration efforts and track progress over time. This may involve tracking metrics such as the number of risk assessments conducted, the level of risk awareness among employees, or the percentage of processes with embedded risk controls to assess the maturity and effectiveness of risk management integration initiatives. By monitoring these metrics, organizations can identify areas for improvement, address gaps in risk management processes, and demonstrate the value of risk management integration to stakeholders and senior leadership.

Additionally, organizations may conduct periodic reviews and audits of integrated risk management processes to ensure alignment with organizational objectives, regulatory requirements, and industry best practices. This may involve evaluating the effectiveness of risk controls, assessing the adequacy of risk management documentation, and identifying opportunities for process optimization or enhancement. By conducting regular reviews and audits, organizations can identify emerging risks, address deficiencies in risk management processes, and continuously improve their risk management capabilities.

In summary, integrating risk management into business processes is essential for organizations to proactively identify, assess, and manage risks across their operations and decision-making processes. By embedding risk management practices directly within existing workflows, leveraging technology-enabled solutions, and fostering a culture of risk awareness and accountability, organizations can enhance resilience, optimize decision-making, and achieve their objectives in an increasingly complex and uncertain business environment.

Chapter 7: Integrating Risk Management with Business Continuity Planning

The relationship between risk management and business continuity is symbiotic, with each discipline complementing and reinforcing the other in safeguarding organizational resilience and continuity of operations. Risk management encompasses the identification, assessment, and mitigation of potential risks that may impact an organization's objectives, assets, or operations. This proactive approach to risk management enables organizations to anticipate and address potential threats and vulnerabilities before they materialize, reducing the likelihood and severity of adverse impacts. One common risk management technique is the use of risk registers, which serve as repositories for cataloging and prioritizing risks based on their likelihood and potential impact. By maintaining risk registers, organizations can systematically track and manage risks across various areas of their operations, facilitating informed decision-making and risk prioritization.

Moreover, risk management extends beyond the identification and assessment of risks to include the implementation of risk mitigation strategies and controls to reduce exposure and minimize potential losses. This may involve implementing technical controls, such as firewalls or intrusion detection systems, to mitigate cybersecurity risks, or developing business continuity plans to ensure continuity of critical operations in the event of a disruption. Business continuity planning is a key component of risk management, focusing on the development and implementation of strategies and procedures to maintain essential functions and services during and after a disruptive event.

One essential aspect of business continuity planning is the identification and prioritization of critical business processes and resources that are essential for maintaining operations and delivering key services. This involves conducting business impact analyses (BIAs) to assess the potential consequences of disruptions to these processes and resources and prioritize recovery efforts accordingly. By understanding the interdependencies between different business functions and resources, organizations can develop targeted business continuity strategies to minimize the impact of disruptions on critical operations and ensure timely recovery.

Moreover, organizations may implement redundant systems or backup facilities to mitigate the risk of single points of failure and ensure resilience in the face of disruptions. For example, organizations may deploy redundant data centers or cloud-based infrastructure to maintain data availability and accessibility in the event of a system outage or failure. Additionally, organizations may establish alternate work sites or telecommuting capabilities to enable employees to continue working remotely during emergencies, ensuring continuity of operations even when primary facilities are unavailable.

Furthermore, organizations may conduct regular exercises and drills to test the effectiveness of their business continuity plans and identify areas for improvement. This may involve tabletop exercises, simulated scenarios, or full-scale emergency response drills to evaluate the readiness and responsiveness of employees and stakeholders during a crisis. By conducting these exercises, organizations can identify gaps in their business continuity plans, refine response procedures, and enhance overall preparedness for emergencies.

Additionally, risk management and business continuity planning require ongoing monitoring and review to ensure their continued effectiveness and relevance in the face of evolving threats and changing business environments. This may involve regular updates to risk registers and business impact analyses to reflect new risks or changes in organizational priorities, as well as periodic reviews of business continuity plans to incorporate lessons learned from past incidents or exercises. By maintaining a proactive and adaptive approach to risk management and business continuity, organizations can enhance their resilience and agility in the face of uncertainty and disruption, enabling them to navigate challenges and sustain long-term success.

In summary, the relationship between risk management and business continuity is essential for organizations to effectively identify, assess, and mitigate risks while maintaining continuity of operations during and after disruptions. By integrating risk management practices with business continuity planning, organizations can develop comprehensive strategies and procedures to anticipate and respond to threats, safeguarding organizational resilience and ensuring the delivery of critical services and functions. Developing business continuity plans (BCPs) based on risk assessments is a critical process for organizations aiming to mitigate the impact of potential disruptions and ensure continuity of operations in adverse scenarios. The first step in this process is conducting a comprehensive risk assessment to identify and evaluate potential threats and vulnerabilities that may affect the organization's ability to operate effectively. This may involve leveraging risk assessment methodologies such as qualitative risk analysis, quantitative risk analysis, or scenario-based assessments to systematically identify and prioritize risks based on their likelihood and potential impact. One commonly used technique for conducting risk assessments is the use of risk matrices, which provide a visual representation of the likelihood and severity of identified risks, enabling organizations to prioritize risk management efforts accordingly.

Once risks have been identified and assessed, organizations can begin developing BCPs to address potential disruptions and ensure continuity of critical operations. BCPs are comprehensive documents that outline the strategies, procedures, and resources required to maintain essential functions and services during and after a disruptive event. These plans typically include sections addressing key components such as emergency response procedures, business impact analyses (BIAs), recovery strategies, and communication protocols.

Emergency response procedures outline the steps employees should take in the event of an emergency or crisis, including evacuation procedures, emergency contacts, and protocols for reporting incidents. These procedures are essential for ensuring the safety and well-being of employees and stakeholders during emergencies and facilitating a coordinated response to mitigate the impact of disruptions.

Business impact analyses (BIAs) are another crucial component of BCPs, providing insights into the potential consequences of disruptions to critical business processes and resources. BIAs involve assessing the financial, operational, and reputational impacts of disruptions and prioritizing recovery efforts based on the criticality of affected functions and services. By conducting BIAs, organizations can identify dependencies, interdependencies, and recovery time objectives (RTOs) for critical processes, enabling them to develop targeted recovery strategies and allocate resources effectively.

Recovery strategies outline the actions and measures organizations will take to restore critical functions and services following a disruptive event. These strategies may include backup and recovery procedures, alternative work arrangements, or relocation plans to ensure continuity of operations. For example, organizations may implement redundant systems, backup facilities, or cloud-based infrastructure to maintain data availability and accessibility in the event of a system outage or failure.

Communication protocols are also essential components of BCPs, enabling organizations to disseminate critical information and instructions to employees, stakeholders, and external partners during emergencies. These protocols outline the channels, procedures, and roles and responsibilities for communicating with internal and external stakeholders, facilitating timely and effective communication during crises.

Moreover, BCPs should be regularly reviewed, updated, and tested to ensure their effectiveness and relevance in the face of evolving threats and changing business environments. This may involve conducting tabletop exercises, simulated scenarios, or full-scale emergency response drills to evaluate the readiness and responsiveness of employees and stakeholders during a crisis. By testing BCPs, organizations can identify gaps, weaknesses, and areas for improvement, refine response procedures, and enhance overall preparedness for emergencies.

Additionally, organizations may leverage technology-enabled solutions to facilitate the development, implementation, and maintenance of BCPs. This may include using business continuity planning software platforms like BCP Builder or Assurance Software, which provide features such as plan templates, workflow automation, and reporting capabilities to streamline BCP development and management. By leveraging these platforms, organizations can centralize BCP documentation, track plan updates, and generate real-time reports to inform decision-making and compliance efforts.

In summary, developing BCPs based on risk assessments is essential for organizations to mitigate the impact of potential disruptions and ensure continuity of operations during and after emergencies. By conducting comprehensive risk assessments, developing targeted recovery strategies, and implementing communication protocols, organizations can enhance their resilience and agility in the face of uncertainty and disruption, safeguarding their ability to deliver critical functions and services to stakeholders.

Chapter 8: Role of Risk Management in Compliance and Legal Requirements

Compliance frameworks play a crucial role in facilitating effective risk management practices within organizations, providing structured guidelines and standards to ensure regulatory compliance and mitigate potential risks. One widely adopted compliance framework is the Payment Card Industry Data Security Standard (PCI DSS), which outlines requirements for organizations that handle cardholder data to ensure secure payment card transactions. To adhere to PCI DSS requirements, organizations must implement security controls such as encryption, access controls, and network segmentation to protect cardholder data from unauthorized access or disclosure. Another prominent compliance framework is the Health Insurance Portability and Accountability Act (HIPAA), which sets standards for the protection of sensitive patient health information. Organizations subject to HIPAA regulations must implement administrative, physical, and technical safeguards to safeguard protected health information (PHI) and prevent data breaches or unauthorized disclosures. CLI commands can be used to deploy security controls required by compliance frameworks, such as configuring firewalls, implementing access controls, or encrypting sensitive data. For example, organizations can use CLI commands to configure firewall rules to restrict inbound and outbound traffic to comply with PCI DSS requirements. Similarly, organizations can use CLI commands to enforce access controls by configuring user permissions and authentication mechanisms to restrict access to sensitive data based on the principle of least privilege. Additionally, organizations can use CLI commands to enable encryption for data in transit and at rest to protect sensitive information from unauthorized access or disclosure, thereby aligning with compliance requirements and mitigating the risk of data breaches. Compliance frameworks also provide organizations with a structured approach to risk management by delineating specific requirements and controls to address various risks and vulnerabilities. For example, the National Institute of Standards and Technology (NIST) Cybersecurity Framework offers a risk-based approach to managing cybersecurity risks by providing guidelines and best practices for identifying, protecting, detecting, responding to, and recovering from cyber threats. By aligning with the NIST Cybersecurity Framework, organizations can develop risk management strategies tailored to their specific risk profiles and business objectives, enhancing their resilience to cyber threats and vulnerabilities. Furthermore, compliance frameworks often require organizations to conduct regular risk assessments to identify and prioritize risks, evaluate the effectiveness of existing controls, and implement additional measures to mitigate identified risks. Risk assessments involve assessing the likelihood and potential impact of various threats and vulnerabilities to determine their significance to the organization and prioritize risk management efforts accordingly. Organizations can leverage risk management methodologies and tools to conduct comprehensive risk assessments, such as the use of risk matrices, risk registers, or risk heat maps to systematically identify, assess, and prioritize risks based on their likelihood and potential impact. By integrating risk management practices with compliance frameworks, organizations can establish a holistic approach to managing risks, ensuring regulatory compliance, and enhancing overall security posture. This integrated approach enables organizations to align their risk management efforts with business objectives and regulatory requirements, effectively mitigating risks and safeguarding against potential threats and vulnerabilities. Moreover, compliance frameworks often require organizations to implement controls and measures to monitor and assess compliance with regulatory requirements continuously. This may involve conducting regular audits, assessments, or penetration tests to evaluate the effectiveness of existing controls, identify areas for improvement, and ensure ongoing compliance with regulatory requirements. By establishing robust monitoring and assessment mechanisms, organizations can detect and address compliance gaps proactively, mitigate potential risks, and demonstrate a commitment to regulatory compliance and risk management excellence. Legal implications are a critical consideration in risk management decisions, as organizations must navigate complex regulatory frameworks and legal obligations to mitigate potential liabilities and ensure compliance with applicable laws and regulations. One key legal implication of risk management decisions is the potential for legal liability arising from failure to adequately identify, assess, or mitigate risks that result in harm to individuals, organizations, or the environment. Organizations may face lawsuits, fines, or regulatory sanctions for negligence or non-compliance with legal requirements, highlighting the importance of robust risk management practices to minimize exposure to legal risks. For example, organizations operating in highly regulated industries such as healthcare or finance must adhere to stringent legal requirements and industry standards to protect sensitive data, ensure patient safety, or prevent financial fraud. Failure to comply with these legal requirements can result in severe legal and financial consequences, including legal action, reputational damage, or loss of business opportunities. CLI commands can be used to deploy technical controls and security measures required to comply with legal requirements and mitigate legal risks. For instance, organizations can use CLI commands to configure encryption protocols, access controls, or data retention policies to protect sensitive information and comply with data protection regulations such as the General Data Protection Regulation (GDPR) or the California Consumer Privacy Act (CCPA). Similarly, organizations can use CLI commands to implement security patches, updates, or vulnerability assessments to identify and remediate security vulnerabilities that may expose them to legal risks such as data breaches or cyberattacks. Moreover, legal implications extend beyond regulatory compliance to encompass contractual obligations, industry standards, and common law principles that govern business relationships and transactions. For example, organizations may enter into contracts with third-party vendors or service providers that impose specific legal requirements or security standards to protect sensitive information or intellectual property. Failure to meet these contractual obligations can result in legal disputes, breach of contract claims, or financial penalties, underscoring the importance of effective risk management practices to ensure compliance with contractual commitments and mitigate legal risks. Additionally, risk management decisions may have implications for corporate governance, accountability, and fiduciary duties owed to stakeholders such as shareholders, customers, or employees. Corporate directors and officers have a legal obligation to act in the best interests of the company and its stakeholders, which includes implementing effective risk management strategies to protect the organization's assets, reputation, and long-term viability. Failure to fulfill these fiduciary duties can result in legal action, shareholder lawsuits, or regulatory investigations alleging breach of duty or misconduct. Therefore, organizations must ensure that risk management decisions are aligned with corporate governance principles and legal requirements to mitigate potential legal exposure and uphold ethical standards of conduct. Furthermore, risk management decisions may also have broader societal implications, particularly concerning environmental, social, and governance (ESG) considerations that impact sustainability, corporate responsibility, and stakeholder trust. Organizations face increasing pressure from investors, consumers, and regulators to address ESG risks such as climate change, social inequality, or unethical business practices, which can have legal, financial, and reputational consequences if not adequately managed. By integrating ESG considerations into their risk management processes, organizations can enhance transparency, accountability, and long-term value creation while mitigating legal and reputational risks associated with environmental or social harm. In summary, legal implications are a critical aspect of risk management decisions, requiring organizations to navigate a complex landscape of regulatory requirements, contractual obligations, and corporate governance principles to minimize legal risks and ensure compliance with applicable laws and regulations. By deploying technical controls, adhering to contractual commitments, and upholding fiduciary duties, organizations can mitigate legal exposure, protect stakeholders' interests, and foster trust and confidence in their operations.

Chapter 9: Advanced Topics in Risk Management: Emerging Threats and Trends

The emerging threat landscape presents a dynamic and evolving challenge for organizations across all sectors, as cyber threats continue to evolve in sophistication, scale, and impact. One of the most significant emerging threats is ransomware, a type of malicious software that encrypts files or systems and demands payment for their release. Organizations can deploy endpoint security solutions such as antivirus software or endpoint detection and response (EDR) tools to detect and block ransomware attacks. Additionally, organizations should implement regular backups of critical data and systems to mitigate the risk of data loss or disruption caused by ransomware attacks. Another emerging threat is supply chain attacks, where threat actors target third-party vendors or service providers to gain unauthorized access to an organization's systems or data. Organizations can mitigate the risk of supply chain attacks by conducting thorough due diligence when selecting vendors, implementing strong vendor risk management processes, and monitoring third-party access to sensitive systems and data. Insider threats also pose a significant risk to organizations, as employees or trusted insiders may intentionally or unintentionally compromise sensitive information or systems. Organizations can deploy user behavior analytics (UBA) solutions to monitor and detect anomalous or suspicious behavior indicative of insider threats. Additionally, organizations should implement robust access controls, user authentication mechanisms, and employee training programs to educate employees about security best practices and raise awareness about the risks associated with insider threats. Another emerging threat is the proliferation of Internet of Things (IoT) devices, which present new attack vectors and vulnerabilities that threat actors can exploit to compromise network security. Organizations can mitigate the risk posed by IoT devices by implementing network segmentation, device authentication mechanisms, and regular firmware updates to patch known vulnerabilities and protect against unauthorized access. Additionally, organizations should conduct comprehensive risk assessments to identify and prioritize IoT-related risks and implement security controls accordingly. Advanced persistent threats (APTs) are another emerging threat vector that organizations must contend with, as threat actors use sophisticated techniques to gain persistent access to networks and exfiltrate sensitive data over an extended period. Organizations can deploy network intrusion detection systems (NIDS) or security information and event management (SIEM) solutions to detect and respond to APTs by monitoring network traffic for suspicious activity or indicators of compromise. Additionally, organizations should implement strong access controls, data encryption, and network segmentation to limit the impact of APTs and prevent unauthorized access to sensitive information. Furthermore, the rise of artificial intelligence (AI) and machine learning (ML) technologies introduces new opportunities and challenges in cybersecurity, as threat actors leverage AI-driven techniques to automate attacks, evade detection, and exploit vulnerabilities at scale. Organizations can deploy AI-powered security solutions to enhance threat detection, analyze vast amounts of security data, and identify patterns indicative of malicious activity. Additionally, organizations should invest in AI-driven threat intelligence platforms to gain insights into emerging threats, vulnerabilities, and attack trends and proactively adapt their security posture to mitigate evolving risks. In summary, the emerging threat landscape presents multifaceted challenges for organizations, as cyber threats continue to evolve in complexity, frequency, and severity. By deploying a multi-layered approach to cybersecurity that combines technical controls, employee training, and threat intelligence, organizations can mitigate the risks posed by emerging threats and enhance their resilience to cyber attacks. Proactive risk management strategies are essential for organizations to effectively mitigate the ever-evolving landscape of emerging threats, requiring a comprehensive approach that encompasses prevention, detection, response, and recovery measures. One proactive strategy is to conduct regular risk assessments to identify and prioritize emerging threats based on their likelihood and potential impact on the organization's operations, assets, and reputation. Organizations can deploy risk assessment methodologies such as qualitative risk analysis, quantitative risk analysis, or scenario-based risk assessments to systematically evaluate emerging threats and develop risk mitigation strategies accordingly. Additionally, organizations can leverage threat intelligence feeds and security information and event management (SIEM) solutions to monitor and analyze emerging threats in real-time, enabling proactive threat detection and response. CLI commands such as "grep" can be used to search for specific patterns or indicators of compromise in log files, allowing organizations to identify potential security incidents and take immediate action to mitigate the threat. Furthermore, organizations can implement security controls such as network segmentation, access controls, and encryption to limit the impact of emerging threats and prevent unauthorized access to sensitive information or systems. For example, organizations can use CLI commands to configure firewall rules to restrict inbound and outbound traffic based on predefined security policies, thereby reducing the attack surface and mitigating the risk of network-based attacks. Additionally, organizations can deploy intrusion detection and prevention systems (IDPS) to monitor network traffic for suspicious activity or known attack signatures and take automated action to block or quarantine malicious traffic. Moreover, proactive risk management strategies should include employee training and awareness programs to educate staff about emerging threats, security best practices, and their role in maintaining a secure work environment. Organizations can use CLI commands to conduct phishing simulations or security awareness training sessions to test employees' awareness of common social engineering tactics and educate them about the importance of safeguarding sensitive information. By empowering employees to recognize and report security incidents promptly, organizations can strengthen their overall security posture and minimize the risk of insider threats or human error-related incidents. Additionally, organizations can establish incident response and business continuity plans to ensure a coordinated and effective response to emerging threats and minimize the impact on business operations. CLI commands such as "curl" can be used to retrieve incident response playbooks or runbooks from a centralized repository, providing responders with step-by-step guidance on how to identify, contain, and remediate security incidents. Furthermore, organizations should regularly test and update their incident response and business continuity plans to address evolving threats and ensure readiness to respond effectively to security incidents or disruptions. By conducting tabletop exercises, red team/blue team exercises, or simulated cyber attack scenarios, organizations can validate their incident response capabilities, identify gaps in their processes, and refine their procedures accordingly. Additionally, organizations can leverage threat intelligence sharing platforms and industry collaboration initiatives to exchange information about emerging threats, vulnerabilities, and best practices with peer organizations and security experts. By participating in threat intelligence sharing communities, organizations can gain valuable insights into emerging threats and trends, enabling them to better anticipate and respond to evolving cyber risks. In summary, proactive risk management strategies are essential for organizations to effectively mitigate the ever-evolving landscape of emerging threats, requiring a multifaceted approach that integrates technical controls, employee training, incident response planning, and threat intelligence sharing. By adopting a proactive mindset and staying vigilant against emerging threats, organizations can enhance their resilience to cyber attacks and safeguard their assets, data, and reputation from evolving cyber risks.

Chapter 10: Case Studies and Practical Applications in Risk Management

Real-world risk management scenarios provide valuable insights into the practical application of risk management principles and techniques in various organizational contexts, helping professionals understand how to identify, assess, and mitigate risks effectively. One common real-world scenario is a data breach, where sensitive information such as customer data, intellectual property, or financial records is compromised due to unauthorized access or cyberattack. Organizations can use CLI commands such as "grep" to search for specific patterns or indicators of compromise in log files, helping them identify the source of the breach and take immediate action to contain and remediate the incident. Additionally, organizations should implement incident response plans to guide their response efforts, including communication protocols, stakeholder notifications, and forensic investigations to determine the extent of the breach and prevent further damage. Another real-world scenario is a supply chain disruption, where disruptions to suppliers, vendors, or logistics partners impact an organization's ability to deliver products or services to customers. Organizations can mitigate the risk of supply chain disruptions by conducting supplier risk assessments, diversifying their supplier base, and establishing contingency plans to address potential disruptions such as natural disasters, geopolitical events, or cyberattacks targeting supply chain partners. CLI commands such as "ping" can be used to test network connectivity to critical suppliers or vendors, helping organizations assess the reliability and resilience of their supply chain network. Moreover, organizations should maintain open lines of communication with suppliers and partners to share information about potential risks and collaborate on mitigation strategies to minimize the impact of disruptions on business operations. Additionally, regulatory compliance failures represent a significant risk for organizations, as non-compliance with industry regulations or data protection laws can result in legal penalties, fines, or reputational damage. Organizations can use CLI commands to automate compliance checks, audit trails, or security assessments to ensure continuous compliance with regulatory requirements and identify potential compliance gaps or vulnerabilities. For example, organizations can use configuration management tools such as "ansible" or "puppet" to enforce security configurations and compliance policies across their IT infrastructure, ensuring consistency and adherence to regulatory standards. Furthermore, organizations should establish governance structures and processes to oversee compliance efforts, including regular audits, risk assessments, and employee training programs to educate staff about regulatory requirements and their role in maintaining compliance. Another real-world risk management scenario is a natural disaster, such as a hurricane, earthquake, or flood, which can cause significant disruptions to business operations, infrastructure, and supply chains. Organizations can mitigate the risk of natural disasters by implementing business continuity and disaster recovery plans that outline procedures for responding to and recovering from such events. CLI commands such as "rsync" or "scp" can be used to replicate data and resources to offsite locations or cloud-based storage platforms, ensuring data availability and resilience in the event of a disaster. Additionally, organizations should conduct regular risk assessments to identify vulnerabilities in their infrastructure and facilities, such as single points of failure or critical dependencies, and implement mitigation measures such as redundant systems, backup generators, or alternate work locations to minimize the impact of natural disasters on business operations. Moreover, employee misconduct or unethical behavior represents a significant risk for organizations, as insider threats or malicious actors can compromise sensitive information, sabotage systems, or engage in fraudulent activities that harm the organization's reputation and financial standing. Organizations can use CLI commands to monitor user activity, access logs, or network traffic for suspicious behavior or anomalies that may indicate insider threats or security breaches. For example, organizations can use "awk" or "sed" commands to parse log files and extract relevant information about user logins, file access, or system activities, helping them identify potential security incidents or policy violations. Additionally, organizations should implement user access controls, least privilege principles, and employee monitoring tools to limit the risk of insider threats and detect unauthorized or suspicious behavior in real-time. In summary, real-world risk management scenarios provide valuable opportunities for organizations to apply risk management principles and techniques in practice, helping them identify, assess, and mitigate risks effectively across various operational contexts. By understanding the challenges and complexities of real-world risk scenarios, professionals can develop proactive risk management strategies that enhance resilience, protect assets, and support business continuity in the face of emerging threats and uncertainties. Lessons learned from risk management case studies offer invaluable insights into real-world scenarios where organizations have faced and overcome various challenges related to identifying, assessing, and mitigating risks effectively. One notable case study is the Equifax data breach, which occurred in 2017 when cyber attackers exploited a vulnerability in the company's web application to gain unauthorized access to sensitive personal information of over 147 million individuals. The breach resulted in significant financial losses, regulatory fines, and reputational damage for Equifax, highlighting the importance of proactive vulnerability management and patching processes to mitigate the risk of cyber threats. Organizations can learn from this case study by prioritizing vulnerability management efforts, conducting regular security assessments, and promptly applying patches and updates to address known vulnerabilities in their IT infrastructure. Another instructive case study is the Deepwater Horizon oil spill, one of the largest environmental disasters in history, which occurred in 2010 when an offshore drilling rig operated by BP experienced a catastrophic explosion and subsequent oil leak in the Gulf of Mexico. The disaster resulted in loss of life, extensive environmental damage, and billions of dollars in cleanup costs and legal liabilities for BP, underscoring the importance of effective risk management and contingency planning in high-risk industries such as oil and gas exploration. Organizations can learn from this case study by implementing robust risk assessment processes, conducting comprehensive safety audits, and developing contingency plans to respond to emergencies and minimize the impact of potential disasters on human safety and the environment. Additionally, the Volkswagen emissions scandal serves as a cautionary tale of corporate misconduct and regulatory non-compliance, where the automotive giant deliberately installed software in its diesel vehicles to manipulate emissions test results and deceive regulators and consumers about the true level of air pollution emitted by its vehicles. The scandal resulted in significant financial penalties, lawsuits, and reputational damage for Volkswagen, highlighting the importance of ethical conduct, transparency, and regulatory compliance in corporate governance and risk management. Organizations can learn from this case study by promoting a culture of integrity and accountability, establishing robust compliance programs, and fostering transparency and openness in their interactions with regulators, customers, and stakeholders. Furthermore, the WannaCry ransomware attack, which occurred in 2017, affected hundreds of thousands of computers worldwide by exploiting a vulnerability in Microsoft Windows operating systems and encrypting files for ransom. The attack disrupted critical services, including healthcare systems, transportation networks, and financial institutions, underscoring the importance of cybersecurity awareness, proactive patch management, and incident response preparedness in mitigating the risk of cyber threats. Organizations can learn from this case study by implementing comprehensive cybersecurity measures, such as regular software updates, network segmentation, and employee training programs to prevent, detect, and respond to ransomware attacks effectively. Moreover, the Boeing 737 MAX crisis represents a notable case study of product safety and regulatory oversight failures, where two fatal crashes involving Boeing 737 MAX aircraft raised concerns about design flaws, pilot training, and regulatory oversight in the aviation industry. The crisis resulted in widespread grounding of 737 MAX aircraft, significant financial losses for Boeing, and reputational damage to the company's brand and credibility. Organizations can learn from this case study by prioritizing safety and quality in product development, fostering transparency and collaboration with regulators and industry stakeholders, and implementing robust risk management processes to identify and address potential safety risks in complex systems and technologies. In summary, lessons learned from risk management case studies provide valuable insights and practical guidance for organizations seeking to enhance their risk management practices, prevent costly mistakes, and mitigate the impact of emerging risks and uncertainties. By studying real-world examples of risk management successes and failures, organizations can identify best practices, avoid common pitfalls, and develop proactive strategies to anticipate, assess, and mitigate risks effectively in today's dynamic and interconnected business environment.

BOOK 3
ADVANCED STRATEGIES FOR GOVERNANCE AND COMPLIANCE IN CISM

ROB BOTWRIGHT

Chapter 1: Evolution of Governance in Information Security

Historical perspectives on information security governance provide valuable insights into the evolution of governance structures, principles, and practices over time, tracing the origins of modern governance frameworks and standards back to early attempts to secure information and protect organizational assets. One of the earliest historical examples of information security governance dates back to ancient civilizations such as the Roman Empire, where rulers and military leaders used encryption techniques to secure sensitive communications and protect strategic information from adversaries. For instance, Julius Caesar is famously known for using a simple substitution cipher known as the Caesar cipher to encrypt his military orders and diplomatic correspondence, highlighting the importance of confidentiality and secrecy in safeguarding sensitive information. Organizations can draw parallels from these historical examples by emphasizing the need for encryption and cryptographic techniques to protect sensitive data and communications from unauthorized access and interception. Another historical perspective on information security governance can be traced to the invention of the telegraph in the 19th century, which revolutionized long-distance communication but also introduced new risks and vulnerabilities related to wiretapping and interception of telegraph messages. In response to these threats, governments and private organizations developed cryptographic systems and security protocols to secure telegraph communications and prevent eavesdropping by unauthorized individuals or adversaries. One notable example is the ADFGVX cipher, used by the German military during World War I to encrypt telegraph messages and maintain the secrecy of military communications on the battlefield. Organizations can learn from these historical experiences by recognizing the importance of protecting communication channels and implementing robust encryption protocols to secure sensitive data in transit. Furthermore, the advent of computer technology in the 20th century brought new challenges and opportunities for information security governance, as organizations began to rely on computers and digital systems to store, process, and transmit vast amounts of information. With the proliferation of computer networks and the internet, the need for comprehensive security measures became increasingly apparent, leading to the development of early cybersecurity frameworks and standards such as the Trusted Computer System Evaluation Criteria (TCSEC), also known as the "Orange Book," published by the United States Department of Defense in the 1980s. The TCSEC established a set of security requirements and evaluation criteria for classifying and assessing the security capabilities of computer systems, laying the groundwork for future cybersecurity standards and best practices. Organizations can take inspiration from the historical development of cybersecurity frameworks and standards by adopting a systematic approach to information security governance, including risk management, compliance, and incident response processes, to protect their digital assets and infrastructure from cyber threats. Additionally, the rise of globalization and interconnectedness in the 21st century has further underscored the importance of information security governance in addressing emerging threats and challenges in a rapidly evolving digital landscape. With the increasing reliance on cloud computing, mobile devices, and internet-connected technologies, organizations face new risks related to data privacy, cybercrime, and regulatory compliance, necessitating a proactive and holistic approach to information security governance. Modern governance frameworks such as the ISO/IEC 27000 series provide organizations with a comprehensive set of guidelines and best practices for establishing, implementing, maintaining, and continuously improving an information security management system (ISMS) tailored to their specific needs and objectives. By embracing historical perspectives on information security governance and leveraging modern governance frameworks and standards, organizations can strengthen their cybersecurity posture, build trust with stakeholders, and effectively navigate the complexities of the digital age. In summary, historical perspectives on information security governance offer valuable lessons and insights for organizations seeking to address the challenges of cybersecurity in today's interconnected world. By studying the evolution of governance structures and practices over time, organizations can gain a deeper understanding of the principles and strategies that underpin effective information security governance and apply these lessons to protect their digital assets and mitigate cyber risks effectively. The impact of technological advancements on governance evolution has been profound, shaping the way organizations manage risks, make decisions, and ensure accountability in an increasingly digital world. One significant technological advancement that has influenced governance evolution is the widespread adoption of cloud computing, which has transformed the way organizations store, process, and access data. With the advent of cloud services such as Amazon Web Services (AWS), Microsoft Azure, and Google Cloud Platform, organizations can leverage scalable and cost-effective infrastructure to support their business operations, reducing the need for on-premises hardware and software investments. CLI commands such as "aws s3 cp" or "gcloud compute instances create" enable organizations to deploy and manage cloud resources efficiently, allowing for greater flexibility and agility in meeting changing business demands. Moreover, the proliferation of mobile devices and remote work technologies has expanded the boundaries of organizational governance, allowing employees to access corporate networks and data from anywhere, at any time. Mobile device management (MDM) solutions such as Mobilelron or VMware Workspace ONE enable organizations to enforce security policies, manage device configurations, and protect sensitive data on mobile devices, ensuring compliance with regulatory requirements and safeguarding against cyber threats. Additionally, the rise of artificial intelligence (AI) and machine learning (ML) technologies has introduced new opportunities and challenges for governance evolution, as organizations seek to harness the power of data analytics and automation to improve decision-making and operational efficiency. AI-driven governance tools such as predictive analytics platforms or robotic process automation (RPA) software enable organizations to analyze vast amounts of data, identify trends and patterns, and automate routine tasks, streamlining governance processes and enhancing risk management capabilities. CLI commands such as "python train_model.py" or "docker run -it rpa_tool" facilitate the development and deployment of AI and ML solutions, empowering organizations to leverage advanced technologies for governance innovation. Furthermore, the emergence of blockchain technology has the potential to revolutionize governance practices by providing a decentralized and tamper-proof ledger for recording transactions and ensuring transparency and accountability in business processes. Blockchain-based governance solutions such as smart contracts enable organizations to automate and enforce contractual agreements, verify the integrity of data and transactions, and reduce the risk of fraud or manipulation. CLI commands such as "geth --datadir /path/to/data init genesis.json" or "truffle migrate --network ropsten" allow developers to deploy and interact with blockchain networks, facilitating the implementation of blockchain-based governance solutions. Moreover, the growing importance of data privacy and regulatory compliance has driven organizations to adopt robust governance frameworks and standards to protect consumer privacy and ensure legal compliance. Regulatory compliance management platforms such as OneTrust or

TrustArc enable organizations to assess, monitor, and demonstrate compliance with data protection regulations such as the General Data Protection Regulation (GDPR) or the California Consumer Privacy Act (CCPA). CLI commands such as "docker-compose up -d" or "kubectl apply -f compliance_policy.yaml" facilitate the deployment and configuration of compliance management tools, helping organizations mitigate regulatory risks and maintain trust with customers and stakeholders. In summary, the impact of technological advancements on governance evolution is profound, reshaping the way organizations manage risks, make decisions, and ensure accountability in today's digital age. By embracing innovative technologies such as cloud computing, mobile devices, AI, ML, blockchain, and compliance management platforms, organizations can enhance their governance practices, drive operational excellence, and achieve competitive advantage in an increasingly complex and interconnected business environment.

Chapter 2: Governance Structures and Models

Traditional governance structures have long been the cornerstone of organizational management, providing a framework for decision-making, accountability, and oversight across various levels of an organization. One of the most common traditional governance structures is the hierarchical model, where authority and decision-making power flow from top-level executives down through a series of managerial levels to frontline employees. This hierarchical structure is characterized by clear lines of authority, with each level responsible for specific functions and accountable to higher-level management for performance and results. Another traditional governance structure is the functional model, where departments or functional areas such as finance, marketing, and operations operate as distinct units within the organization, each with its own set of responsibilities and reporting lines. In this model, decision-making is decentralized, with department heads or functional managers exercising authority over their respective areas of expertise. The functional model is often used in large organizations with diverse business operations, allowing for specialization and expertise in different functional areas. Additionally, the matrix governance structure combines elements of both the hierarchical and functional models, allowing for greater flexibility and integration across organizational units. In a matrix structure, employees report to both a functional manager and a project or product manager, enabling cross-functional collaboration and coordination on complex projects or initiatives. This structure is particularly well-suited to organizations operating in dynamic and fast-paced environments, where agility and responsiveness are essential for success. Furthermore, the committee-based governance structure involves the formation of committees or boards comprised of representatives from different organizational functions or stakeholder groups to oversee specific areas of governance, such as risk management, compliance, or strategic planning. Committees may include members from various levels of the organization, as well as external stakeholders such as shareholders, regulators, or industry experts, ensuring a diverse range of perspectives and expertise in decision-making processes. The committee-based structure is often used in nonprofit organizations, government agencies, and corporate boards to provide oversight and governance in areas of strategic importance. Moreover, the centralized governance structure consolidates decision-making authority within a central governing body or executive team, which makes strategic decisions and sets policies that are implemented across the organization. This structure is common in small businesses or startups, where decision-making is concentrated in the hands of a few key individuals or founders, enabling rapid decision-making and execution. However, centralized governance can also lead to inefficiencies and delays in decision-making, particularly in larger organizations where decision-making authority is concentrated at the top and may be disconnected from frontline operations. Conversely, the decentralized governance structure distributes decision-making authority across multiple levels of the organization, empowering frontline employees and managers to make decisions autonomously within their areas of responsibility. This structure fosters innovation, agility, and accountability at the grassroots level, as employees are empowered to respond quickly to customer needs and market changes without waiting for approval from higher-level management. However, decentralized governance can also lead to coordination challenges and inconsistencies in decision-making across different parts of the organization, requiring strong communication and alignment mechanisms to ensure coherence and alignment with organizational goals. Additionally, the network governance structure involves collaboration and coordination among a network of interconnected organizations, stakeholders, and partners to achieve common goals or address shared challenges. This structure is common in industries such as healthcare, education, and environmental conservation, where multiple organizations must work together to deliver services or address complex societal issues. In a network governance model, decision-making authority is distributed among network participants, who collaborate through formal agreements, partnerships, or informal networks to achieve collective outcomes. However, network governance can also pose challenges related to coordination, accountability, and resource allocation, as participants may have divergent interests or priorities that must be reconciled to achieve consensus and drive collective action. Overall, traditional governance structures play a critical role in shaping organizational behavior, decision-making processes, and performance outcomes. By understanding the strengths and limitations of different governance models, organizations can design governance structures that align with their strategic objectives, organizational culture, and external environment, enabling them to navigate complexity, drive innovation, and achieve sustainable growth in today's dynamic and interconnected world. Modern governance models in information security have evolved in response to the dynamic and ever-changing landscape of cyber threats and technological advancements, requiring organizations to adopt innovative approaches to ensure the confidentiality, integrity, and availability of their data and systems. One of the most prominent modern governance models is the risk-based approach, which emphasizes the identification, assessment, and prioritization of cybersecurity risks to inform decision-making and resource allocation. In this model, organizations conduct risk assessments to identify potential threats and vulnerabilities, analyze their potential impact on business operations, and prioritize mitigation efforts based on the level of risk exposure. The National Institute of Standards and Technology (NIST) Cybersecurity Framework provides a comprehensive framework for implementing a risk-based approach to cybersecurity governance, outlining five core functions – Identify, Protect, Detect, Respond, and Recover – that organizations can use to manage cybersecurity risks effectively. The implementation of the NIST Cybersecurity Framework involves a series of steps, including identifying and documenting cybersecurity risks and vulnerabilities, assessing the potential impact of these risks on business operations and objectives, and developing and implementing risk mitigation strategies and controls to reduce the likelihood and impact of cybersecurity incidents. Organizations can use CLI commands such as "nmap -sS -O target" to conduct network scans and identify potential vulnerabilities, "openvpn --config client.ovpn" to establish secure VPN connections for remote access, and "ansible-playbook -i hosts site.yml" to automate the deployment of security controls and configurations across IT infrastructure. Another modern governance model in information security is the zero trust approach, which challenges the traditional perimeter-based security model by assuming that threats may already exist within the network and adopting a more granular and dynamic approach to access control and authentication. In a zero trust model, access to resources and systems is based on the principle of least privilege, with users and devices required to authenticate and authorize themselves before accessing sensitive data or applications. This model relies on technologies such as multi-factor authentication (MFA), identity and access management (IAM), and microsegmentation to enforce access controls and limit the lateral movement of attackers within the network. CLI commands such as "ssh-keygen -t rsa" can be used to generate SSH key pairs for secure authentication, "sudo iptables -A INPUT -s 192.168.1.0/24 -p tcp --dport 22 -j ACCEPT" to configure firewall rules for network segmentation, and "duo-auth -u username" to initiate multi-factor authentication for user login. Additionally, the agile governance model emphasizes flexibility, collaboration, and iterative improvement in managing cybersecurity risks and compliance requirements. In this model, organizations adopt agile principles and practices such as Scrum, Kanban, and DevOps to streamline governance processes, promote cross-functional collaboration, and accelerate the delivery of security controls and updates. Agile governance enables organizations to respond quickly to emerging threats and vulnerabilities, adapt to changing regulatory requirements, and continuously improve their cybersecurity posture through regular feedback and retrospectives. CLI commands such as "git clone repository-url" can be used to clone code repositories for collaborative development, "docker-compose up -d" to deploy containerized applications for testing and production, and "jenkins build project-name" to automate the integration and deployment of software updates. Furthermore, the governance-as-code model leverages infrastructure-as-code (IaC) and configuration management tools to automate the provisioning, configuration, and enforcement of security controls and policies across IT infrastructure and cloud environments. In this model, organizations use code repositories, version control systems, and continuous integration/continuous deployment (CI/CD) pipelines to manage and enforce governance policies as code, ensuring consistency, repeatability, and scalability in governance processes. CLI commands such as "terraform init" can be used to initialize Terraform projects for infrastructure provisioning, "ansible-playbook -i hosts playbook.yml" to automate configuration management tasks, and "kubectl apply -f deployment.yaml" to deploy containerized applications in Kubernetes clusters. Overall, modern governance models in information security are characterized by their agility, adaptability, and emphasis on risk management, access control, and automation. By embracing these models and leveraging technology-driven approaches, organizations can enhance their cybersecurity resilience, meet compliance requirements, and mitigate the evolving threats and challenges of the digital age.

Chapter 3: Regulatory Landscape in Information Security

Information security regulations play a crucial role in shaping the landscape of cybersecurity practices and standards across industries, providing guidelines and requirements for organizations to safeguard sensitive data, protect against cyber threats, and ensure compliance with legal and regulatory obligations. One of the most significant information security regulations is the General Data Protection Regulation (GDPR), enacted by the European Union (EU) to protect the privacy and personal data of EU citizens and residents. The GDPR imposes strict requirements on organizations that process personal data, including consent mechanisms, data breach notification obligations, and accountability measures such as data protection impact assessments (DPIAs) and data protection by design and by default. Compliance with the GDPR requires organizations to implement robust data protection measures, such as encryption, access controls, and data minimization, to mitigate the risks of data breaches and unauthorized access. Another prominent information security regulation is the Health Insurance Portability and Accountability Act (HIPAA), which governs the security and privacy of protected health information (PHI) in the United States. HIPAA establishes standards for the electronic transmission of PHI, requiring healthcare organizations and their business associates to implement administrative, physical, and technical safeguards to protect against unauthorized access, disclosure, and misuse of sensitive patient data. CLI commands such as "hipaa-audit-checks --type technical" can be used to perform technical assessments of HIPAA compliance controls, "openssl enc -aes256 -in file.txt -out file.txt.enc" to encrypt sensitive files containing PHI, and "aws s3 cp file.txt.enc s3://hipaa-compliance-bucket" to securely transfer encrypted files to HIPAA-compliant storage buckets in the Amazon Web Services (AWS) cloud. Additionally, the Payment Card Industry Data Security Standard (PCI DSS) sets requirements for securing payment card data and preventing credit card fraud, applying to organizations that store, process, or transmit cardholder data. PCI DSS mandates the implementation of controls such as network segmentation, encryption, and vulnerability management to protect cardholder data and maintain compliance with industry standards. Compliance with the PCI DSS involves regular assessments and audits to validate adherence to security requirements and identify areas for improvement. CLI commands such as "pcidss-scan --scan-type external" can be used to conduct external vulnerability scans of network infrastructure, "openssl s_client -connect server:443" to verify SSL/TLS certificate configurations for secure transmission of cardholder data, and "nmap --script ssl-enum-ciphers -p 443 server" to assess SSL/TLS cipher suite configurations for compliance with PCI DSS requirements. Furthermore, regulatory frameworks such as the Federal Information Security Management Act (FISMA) in the United States and the Cybersecurity Maturity Model Certification (CMMC) for defense contractors establish standards and requirements for securing federal information systems and protecting sensitive government data. FISMA requires federal agencies to develop, implement, and maintain risk-based information security programs, including security controls, continuous monitoring, and incident response capabilities, to safeguard against cyber threats and vulnerabilities. Similarly, CMMC requires defense contractors and subcontractors to achieve specific levels of cybersecurity maturity and certification to bid on and fulfill Department of Defense (DoD) contracts. Compliance with FISMA and CMMC involves conducting security assessments, implementing recommended security controls, and obtaining third-party certifications to demonstrate compliance with regulatory requirements. CLI commands such as "fisma-assessment-tool --level high" can be used to assess the effectiveness of security controls and practices against FISMA high-level requirements, "cmmc-certification-checklist --level 3" to evaluate compliance with CMMC Level 3 security controls and practices, and "nist-sp800-53 --control AC-2" to reference specific security controls from the NIST Special Publication 800-53 catalog for FISMA compliance. Additionally, sector-specific regulations such as the Federal Financial Institutions Examination Council (FFIEC) guidelines for financial institutions, the Federal Energy Regulatory Commission (FERC) standards for the energy sector, and the National Institute of Standards and Technology (NIST) cybersecurity framework provide industry-specific guidance and best practices for managing cybersecurity risks and protecting critical infrastructure. Compliance with sector-specific regulations requires organizations to assess their unique risks and vulnerabilities, implement appropriate security controls and safeguards, and demonstrate compliance through audits, assessments, and reporting mechanisms. CLI commands such as "ffiec-compliance-check --sector banking" can be used to assess compliance with FFIEC cybersecurity requirements for banking institutions, "ferc-security-standards --sector energy" to evaluate compliance with FERC cybersecurity standards for energy sector entities, and "nist-cybersecurity-framework --sector healthcare" to align with NIST cybersecurity framework recommendations for healthcare organizations. Overall, information security regulations provide a framework for organizations to establish and maintain effective cybersecurity programs, protect sensitive data and critical assets, and mitigate the risks of cyber threats and attacks. By understanding and adhering to regulatory requirements, organizations can enhance their security posture, build trust with stakeholders, and achieve compliance with legal and industry standards in today's complex and interconnected digital environment. Compliance requirements in different jurisdictions present a complex and multifaceted landscape for organizations operating in today's globalized economy, necessitating a comprehensive understanding of legal and regulatory frameworks across various regions and industries. One of the fundamental challenges organizations face is navigating the diverse array of compliance obligations imposed by national, regional, and international laws, which may vary significantly in scope, applicability, and enforcement mechanisms. For example, the European Union's General Data Protection Regulation (GDPR) sets stringent requirements for the protection of personal data and privacy rights, applying to organizations that process or control the personal data of EU residents, regardless of their physical location or headquarters. Compliance with the GDPR entails implementing data protection measures such as pseudonymization, encryption, and data minimization, as well as establishing mechanisms for obtaining consent, notifying data breaches, and facilitating data subject rights. CLI commands such as "gdpr-compliance-check --scope global" can be used to assess organizational readiness and compliance with GDPR requirements, "openssl enc -aes256 -in file.txt -out file.txt.enc" to encrypt personal data files for storage or transmission, and "gdpr-report-generator --period quarterly" to generate compliance reports for regulatory authorities. Similarly, the California Consumer Privacy Act (CCPA) imposes obligations on businesses that collect, process, or sell the personal information of California residents, providing consumers with rights such as the right to access, delete, and opt-out of the sale of their personal data. Compliance with the CCPA requires organizations to implement privacy policies, procedures, and controls to ensure transparency, accountability, and consumer choice in the handling of personal information. CLI commands such as "ccpa-compliance-check --scope statewide" can be used to evaluate organizational compliance with CCPA requirements, "python ccpa-data-deletion-script.py" to automate the deletion of consumer data upon request, and "ccpa-data-privacy-impact-assessment --system CRM" to conduct privacy impact assessments for systems handling personal information. Moreover, the Health Insurance Portability and Accountability Act (HIPAA) in the United States mandates stringent safeguards for protecting the privacy and security of protected health information (PHI) held by covered entities and their business associates. HIPAA requirements include administrative, physical, and technical safeguards to ensure the confidentiality, integrity, and availability of PHI, as well as breach notification requirements and penalties for non-compliance. Compliance with HIPAA involves implementing security measures such as access controls, encryption, and audit trails to safeguard PHI and mitigate the risks of unauthorized access or disclosure. CLI commands such as "hipaa-compliance-audit --scope national" can be used to assess organizational compliance with HIPAA security requirements, "openssl s_client -connect server:443" to verify SSL/TLS configurations for secure transmission of PHI, and "hipaa-breach-notification-template --incident-type unauthorized-access" to generate breach notification letters for affected individuals. Additionally, the Payment Card Industry Data Security Standard (PCI DSS) establishes security requirements for organizations that handle credit card data, aiming to prevent payment card fraud and protect cardholder information. PCI DSS compliance involves implementing controls such as network segmentation, encryption, and vulnerability management to secure payment card data and comply with industry standards. CLI commands such as "pci-dss-compliance-scan --scope merchant" can be used to conduct vulnerability scans and assessments for PCI DSS compliance, "openssl req - new -key server.key -out server.csr" to generate certificate signing requests (CSRs) for SSL/TLS certificates, and "pci-dss-penetration-testing -- scope e-commerce-platform" to perform penetration testing of e-commerce platforms to identify and remediate security vulnerabilities. Moreover, international standards such as ISO/IEC 27001 provide a framework for establishing, implementing, maintaining, and continually improving an information security management system (ISMS) to protect sensitive information and manage security risks effectively. ISO/IEC 27001 certification demonstrates an organization's commitment to information security best practices and compliance with globally recognized standards. Compliance with ISO/IEC 27001 involves conducting risk assessments, implementing security controls, and undergoing audits and certification assessments by accredited certification bodies. CLI commands such as "iso27001-compliance-assessment --scope enterprise-wide" can be used to assess organizational compliance with ISO/IEC 27001 requirements, "ansible-playbook -i hosts security-controls.yml" to automate the deployment of security controls and configurations, and "iso27001-certification-preparation --audit-readiness" to prepare for ISO/IEC 27001 certification audits. In summary, compliance requirements in different jurisdictions present complex challenges for organizations, requiring a proactive and systematic approach to understand, interpret, and address regulatory obligations effectively. By leveraging technology, automation, and best practices, organizations can navigate the regulatory landscape, mitigate compliance risks, and demonstrate their commitment to protecting sensitive data and maintaining the trust of stakeholders in an increasingly regulated environment.

Chapter 4: Compliance Frameworks and Standards

Major compliance frameworks play a pivotal role in guiding organizations across various industries to establish and maintain effective governance, risk management, and compliance programs. One of the most widely recognized compliance frameworks is the Payment Card Industry Data Security Standard (PCI DSS), which is designed to protect cardholder data and ensure secure payment card transactions. Organizations that process, store, or transmit payment card information must comply with PCI DSS requirements to safeguard sensitive data and mitigate the risk of data breaches. PCI DSS compliance involves implementing security controls such as network segmentation, encryption, and access controls to protect cardholder data from unauthorized access or disclosure. Another prominent compliance framework is the Health Insurance Portability and Accountability Act (HIPAA), which sets standards for the protection of sensitive health information and governs the privacy and security practices of healthcare organizations and their business associates. HIPAA compliance entails implementing administrative, physical, and technical safeguards to safeguard protected health information (PHI) and ensure patient privacy rights are upheld. Organizations subject to HIPAA regulations must adhere to requirements such as conducting risk assessments, implementing access controls, and implementing breach notification procedures in the event of a data breach. Additionally, the General Data Protection Regulation (GDPR) is a comprehensive privacy law that governs the processing and protection of personal data of individuals within the European Union (EU) and the European Economic Area (EEA). GDPR compliance is mandatory for organizations that collect, process, or store personal data of EU residents, regardless of their location or headquarters. To achieve GDPR compliance, organizations must implement measures such as obtaining consent for data processing, implementing data protection by design and by default, and ensuring the security and integrity of personal data through appropriate technical and organizational measures. Another significant compliance framework is the Sarbanes-Oxley Act (SOX), which was enacted to enhance corporate governance and financial reporting transparency in publicly traded companies. SOX compliance requires organizations to establish internal controls and procedures to ensure the accuracy and reliability of financial reporting, as well as to prevent fraudulent activities and misconduct. Compliance with SOX involves implementing controls such as segregation of duties, financial reporting controls, and whistleblower protection mechanisms to promote accountability and transparency in corporate governance. Furthermore, the ISO/IEC 27001 standard is an internationally recognized framework for information security management systems (ISMS), providing a systematic approach to managing sensitive information and mitigating security risks. Organizations seeking ISO/IEC 27001 certification must establish, implement, maintain, and continually improve an ISMS to protect confidentiality, integrity, and availability of information assets. ISO/IEC 27001 compliance involves conducting risk assessments, implementing security controls, and undergoing regular audits to ensure compliance with the standard's requirements. In summary, major compliance frameworks serve as essential guidelines for organizations to meet regulatory requirements, protect sensitive data, and uphold ethical standards in their operations. By adhering to these frameworks and implementing appropriate controls and measures, organizations can mitigate compliance risks, enhance trust with stakeholders, and maintain a strong reputation in the marketplace. Implementing industry standards for compliance is crucial for organizations aiming to establish robust governance, risk management, and compliance (GRC) frameworks tailored to their specific regulatory obligations and operational needs. One of the primary steps in implementing industry standards for compliance is to conduct a thorough assessment of the organization's regulatory landscape, identifying applicable laws, regulations, and industry-specific standards that govern its operations. This assessment helps organizations prioritize their compliance efforts and allocate resources effectively to address the most critical compliance requirements. Once the regulatory landscape is understood, organizations can begin the process of aligning their policies, procedures, and controls with relevant industry standards. For example, organizations in the healthcare sector may need to adhere to standards such as the Health Insurance Portability and Accountability Act (HIPAA) or the Health Information Trust Alliance (HITRUST) framework to protect patient data and ensure compliance with healthcare regulations. Similarly, financial institutions may need to comply with standards such as the Payment Card Industry Data Security Standard (PCI DSS) or the Sarbanes-Oxley Act (SOX) to safeguard financial data and uphold transparency and accountability in financial reporting. Implementing industry standards for compliance often involves a combination of technical, administrative, and operational measures to address various aspects of regulatory requirements. For instance, organizations may need to implement access controls, encryption, and audit trails to protect sensitive data, while also establishing policies and procedures for risk management, incident response, and employee training. CLI commands such as "docker run --rm -v $(pwd):/tmp/ burp-scan -u http://example.com -s" can be used to conduct vulnerability scans for web applications to assess compliance with security standards such as OWASP or NIST. Additionally, organizations may leverage automation tools and platforms to streamline compliance processes and ensure consistency and accuracy in compliance activities. For example, configuration management tools like Ansible or Puppet can be used to automate the deployment and configuration of security controls across IT infrastructure, while compliance management platforms like Qualys or Tenable can provide centralized visibility and reporting for compliance efforts. Moreover, organizations must establish mechanisms for monitoring and enforcing compliance with industry standards on an ongoing basis. This includes conducting regular audits, assessments, and reviews of compliance controls and processes to identify gaps or deficiencies and take corrective actions as needed. CLI commands such as "auditctl -w /etc/passwd -p wa -k passwd_changes" can be used to monitor changes to critical system files for compliance with security standards like ISO/IEC

27001. Additionally, organizations may implement incident response and escalation procedures to address non-compliance issues promptly and effectively, mitigating potential risks and liabilities associated with regulatory violations. Furthermore, maintaining documentation and records of compliance activities is essential for demonstrating adherence to industry standards and regulatory requirements. This includes keeping records of policies, procedures, risk assessments, audit reports, and training documentation to provide evidence of compliance efforts to regulators, auditors, and other stakeholders. By documenting compliance activities comprehensively, organizations can demonstrate their commitment to compliance and reduce the likelihood of penalties or fines resulting from non-compliance. In summary, implementing industry standards for compliance is a multifaceted process that requires proactive planning, diligent execution, and continuous monitoring and improvement. By aligning with industry best practices and regulatory requirements, organizations can strengthen their compliance posture, mitigate risks, and foster trust and confidence among customers, partners, and regulators.

Chapter 5: Developing Effective Governance Policies and Procedures

Principles of policy development are fundamental guidelines that organizations follow to create effective and comprehensive policies governing various aspects of their operations. These principles serve as a framework for designing policies that align with the organization's objectives, values, and regulatory requirements. One of the primary principles of policy development is clarity, ensuring that policies are clear, concise, and easily understandable by all stakeholders. This involves using simple language, avoiding jargon or technical terms, and providing examples or explanations where necessary to enhance comprehension. Another important principle is relevance, which requires policies to address current issues, risks, and challenges faced by the organization. Policies should be based on thorough risk assessments and analysis of internal and external factors that may impact the organization's operations. CLI commands such as "grep -r 'policy' /etc/" can be used to search for existing policies or policy-related documents within system files to assess their relevance and applicability. Additionally, policies should be consistent with the organization's values, culture, and ethical standards. They should reflect the organization's commitment to integrity, transparency, and accountability in its conduct and decision-making processes. Consistency ensures that policies are applied uniformly across the organization, avoiding confusion or ambiguity regarding expectations and requirements. Moreover, policies should be comprehensive, covering all relevant areas and aspects of the organization's operations. This includes policies related to information security, privacy, ethics, compliance, human resources, and other key areas that impact organizational performance and reputation. CLI commands such as "ls -l /etc/policies/" can be used to list all policy files stored in a specific directory for review and analysis. Furthermore, policies should be periodically reviewed and updated to ensure their continued effectiveness and relevance in light of changing circumstances, regulations, and business requirements. This involves conducting regular audits and assessments of policies to identify gaps, inconsistencies, or areas for improvement. CLI commands such as "find /etc/policies/ -type f -mtime +365 -exec ls -l {} \;" can be used to find policy files that have not been modified in over a year, indicating the need for review and potential updates. Additionally, policies should be communicated effectively to all relevant stakeholders, including employees, contractors, suppliers, and partners. This ensures that everyone is aware of their rights, responsibilities, and obligations under the policies and understands the consequences of non-compliance. Communication may involve training sessions, employee handbooks, intranet portals, email notifications, or other channels depending on the organization's size and structure. Moreover, organizations should establish mechanisms for monitoring and enforcing compliance with policies, including regular audits, inspections, and disciplinary actions for violations. This helps maintain accountability and integrity within the organization and fosters a culture of compliance and ethical behavior. CLI commands such as "auditctl -w /etc/policies -p rwxa -k policy_changes" can be used to monitor changes to policy files and detect unauthorized modifications or access attempts. Additionally, organizations should provide channels for feedback and suggestions regarding policies, allowing stakeholders to contribute to their improvement and refinement over time. By following these principles of policy development, organizations can create robust, effective, and adaptable policies that support their objectives, values, and regulatory compliance requirements while promoting transparency, accountability, and ethical conduct across the organization. Designing governance procedures for effectiveness is a critical aspect of organizational management, ensuring that governance structures and processes are designed to achieve their intended objectives and deliver value to the organization. One key consideration in designing governance procedures is alignment with organizational goals and objectives. This involves ensuring that governance procedures are closely linked to the organization's strategic direction, mission, and vision. CLI commands such as "grep -r 'mission' /etc/" can be used to search for references to the organization's mission statement within system files to ensure alignment with governance procedures. Additionally, governance procedures should be designed to promote transparency and accountability throughout the organization. This includes establishing clear lines of responsibility, decision-making authority, and reporting mechanisms to ensure that stakeholders are aware of their roles and obligations. Transparency can be enhanced by providing access to governance documentation, meeting minutes, and other relevant information to stakeholders. Furthermore, governance procedures should be designed with flexibility in mind to accommodate changes in the organization's environment, such as shifts in regulatory requirements, market conditions, or technological advancements. This flexibility allows governance procedures to adapt and evolve over time to remain effective and relevant. CLI commands such as "ls -l /etc/governance/" can be used to list governance-related files stored in a specific directory for review and analysis. Moreover, governance procedures should be designed to promote collaboration and communication among stakeholders across the organization. This may involve establishing cross-functional committees, task forces, or working groups to address governance issues and facilitate decision-making. Collaboration can be fostered through regular meetings, workshops, and forums where stakeholders can exchange ideas, share best practices, and address common challenges. Additionally, governance procedures should include mechanisms for monitoring and evaluating their effectiveness. This may involve establishing key performance indicators (KPIs), benchmarks, or metrics to assess the impact of governance procedures on organizational performance and outcomes. CLI commands such as "grep -r 'KPI' /etc/governance/" can be used to search for references to key performance indicators within governance-related documents for evaluation. Furthermore, regular audits, assessments, and reviews can be conducted to identify areas for improvement and ensure compliance with governance standards and regulatory requirements. These audits can be performed using tools and frameworks such as ISO 27001 or COBIT, which provide guidelines for evaluating governance processes and controls. Additionally, governance procedures should be designed with a focus on risk management to identify, assess, and mitigate risks that may impact the achievement of organizational objectives. This involves integrating risk management principles and practices into governance frameworks to ensure that risks are effectively managed and monitored. CLI commands such as "auditctl -w /etc/governance -p wa -k governance_changes" can be used to monitor changes to governance-related files and detect unauthorized modifications or access attempts. Moreover, governance procedures should be regularly reviewed and updated to reflect changes in the organization's internal and external environment. This may involve conducting periodic reviews of governance documentation, policies, and procedures to ensure their continued relevance and effectiveness. CLI commands such as "find /etc/governance/ -type f -mtime +365 -exec ls -l {} \;" can be used to find governance-related files that have not been modified in over a year, indicating the need for review and potential updates. By designing governance procedures for effectiveness, organizations can establish robust frameworks for decision-making, accountability, and risk management that support their strategic objectives and foster sustainable growth and success.

Chapter 6: Implementing Governance Controls and Mechanisms

Governance control frameworks are essential tools that organizations utilize to establish and maintain effective governance practices across various aspects of their operations. These frameworks provide a structured approach for defining, implementing, and monitoring governance controls to ensure compliance with regulatory requirements, mitigate risks, and promote accountability. One prominent governance control framework widely used by organizations worldwide is the Control Objectives for Information and Related Technology (COBIT) framework. COBIT provides a comprehensive set of principles, practices, and guidelines for governing and managing information technology (IT) assets and processes within an organization. It offers a holistic approach to governance by aligning IT objectives with business goals, defining control objectives, and providing a framework for assessing and improving IT governance maturity levels. CLI commands such as "cobit --help" can be used to access the command-line interface for the COBIT framework and explore available options for implementing governance controls. Another widely adopted governance control framework is the Committee of Sponsoring

Organizations of the Treadway Commission (COSO) framework. COSO provides a framework for designing, implementing, and evaluating internal control systems to mitigate risks, achieve operational effectiveness, and ensure compliance with regulations. It consists of five interrelated components: control environment, risk assessment, control activities, information and communication, and monitoring. CLI commands such as "coso -list" can be used to list the components of the COSO framework and explore their interrelationships. Additionally, organizations may adopt industry-specific governance control frameworks tailored to their unique requirements and regulatory environments. For example, the Payment Card Industry Data Security Standard (PCI DSS) provides a framework for securing payment card transactions and protecting cardholder data. It outlines specific requirements for organizations that handle payment card information, including maintaining secure networks, implementing access control measures, and regularly monitoring and testing security systems. CLI commands such as "pcidss --requirements" can be used to access the command-line interface for the PCI DSS framework and review its compliance requirements. Moreover, governance control frameworks often incorporate internationally recognized standards and best practices to ensure alignment with global governance principles and regulatory requirements. For instance, the International Organization for Standardization (ISO) develops standards such as ISO/IEC 27001 for information security management systems (ISMS) and ISO 38500 for IT governance. These standards provide guidelines and requirements for implementing governance controls and managing risks related to information security and IT governance. CLI commands such as "iso27001 --requirements" can be used to access the command-line interface for the ISO/IEC 27001 standard and review its requirements for establishing an ISMS. Furthermore, governance control frameworks facilitate continuous improvement by establishing mechanisms for monitoring, measuring, and evaluating governance controls' effectiveness. This includes conducting regular assessments, audits, and reviews to identify gaps, weaknesses, and opportunities for enhancement. CLI commands such as "auditctl -w /etc/governance -p wa -k governance_changes" can be used to monitor changes to governance-related files and detect unauthorized modifications or access attempts. By implementing governance control frameworks, organizations can establish robust governance practices, mitigate risks, enhance compliance, and achieve their strategic objectives effectively. Automation and tools play a pivotal role in implementing governance practices within organizations, streamlining processes, enhancing efficiency, and ensuring compliance with regulatory requirements. One widely used automation tool is Ansible, which enables organizations to automate various IT tasks, including configuration management, application deployment, and infrastructure provisioning. Ansible employs a simple, agentless architecture that uses SSH to execute commands on remote systems, making it highly scalable and easy to deploy. CLI commands such as "ansible-playbook site.yml" can be used to execute Ansible playbooks, which contain sets of instructions for automating tasks across multiple systems. Additionally, Ansible provides modules for interacting with cloud platforms, enabling organizations to automate cloud infrastructure management tasks such as provisioning, scaling, and configuration. Another popular automation tool is Puppet, which automates IT infrastructure management tasks by defining and enforcing desired system configurations using code. Puppet uses a declarative language called Puppet DSL to describe system states and dependencies, allowing administrators to specify desired configurations and ensure consistency across their infrastructure. CLI commands such as "puppet apply manifest.pp" can be used to apply Puppet manifests, which contain configuration instructions for managing system resources. Furthermore, Puppet offers a rich ecosystem of modules and integrations for managing various technologies and platforms, including cloud environments, containers, and networking devices. Another notable automation tool is Chef, which automates infrastructure management tasks using a domain-specific language (DSL) called Chef Infra. Chef allows administrators to define infrastructure configurations as code, facilitating the automation of provisioning, configuration, and application deployment processes. CLI commands such as "chef-client -- local-mode" can be used to run Chef recipes, which contain instructions for configuring and managing system resources. Additionally, Chef provides a centralized server-client architecture that enables organizations to manage configurations across distributed infrastructure environments efficiently. Moreover, automation tools such as Terraform enable organizations to provision and manage cloud infrastructure resources using code. Terraform uses a declarative configuration language to define infrastructure components, allowing administrators to create, modify, and destroy cloud resources programmatically. CLI commands such as "terraform apply" can be used to apply Terraform configuration files, which describe the desired state of cloud infrastructure resources. Additionally, Terraform supports integration with various cloud providers, enabling organizations to automate infrastructure management tasks across multi-cloud environments. Furthermore, automation tools can be leveraged to enforce governance policies and compliance standards across IT infrastructure environments. For example, tools like Chef InSpec enable organizations to define and enforce security and compliance policies as code, allowing administrators to assess and remediate configuration drifts and vulnerabilities automatically. CLI commands such as "inspec exec controls" can be used to execute Chef InSpec profiles, which contain compliance checks and controls for evaluating system configurations. Additionally, automation tools can be integrated with continuous integration and continuous deployment (CI/CD) pipelines to automate governance checks and validations as part of the software development lifecycle. By incorporating automation and tools into governance implementation processes, organizations can streamline operations, enhance agility, and ensure consistency and compliance across their IT infrastructure environments.

Chapter 7: Auditing and Assessing Governance and Compliance

Audit methodologies are fundamental frameworks utilized by organizations to assess the effectiveness of governance practices and ensure compliance with regulatory requirements, industry standards, and internal policies. One widely adopted audit methodology is the Control Objectives for Information and Related Technology (COBIT) framework, which provides a comprehensive set of principles and practices for evaluating and improving IT governance processes. COBIT defines a structured approach to conducting audits by outlining key control objectives, control practices, and maturity models that organizations can use to assess their governance and compliance posture. Another prominent audit methodology is the International Organization for Standardization (ISO) 27001 standard, which specifies requirements for establishing, implementing, maintaining, and continuously improving an information security management system (ISMS). ISO 27001 audits focus on evaluating the organization's adherence to established policies, procedures, and controls for managing information security risks. Additionally, ISO 27001 audits assess the effectiveness of risk management processes, security controls, and compliance with regulatory requirements. Organizations often conduct ISO 27001 audits using a combination of internal audits, third-party assessments, and certification audits to validate compliance with the standard. Moreover, organizations may employ industry-specific audit methodologies tailored to their sector's regulatory requirements and operational characteristics. For example, financial institutions may utilize audit methodologies such as the Statement on Standards for Attestation Engagements (SSAE) No. 18, developed by the American Institute of Certified Public Accountants (AICPA), to assess the effectiveness of internal controls over financial reporting. SSAE 18 audits focus on evaluating the design and operating effectiveness of controls relevant to financial reporting and regulatory compliance. Furthermore, organizations may conduct risk-based audits to prioritize audit activities and allocate resources effectively based on the significance and potential impact of identified risks. Risk-based audit methodologies involve assessing the likelihood and impact of risks on organizational objectives, identifying control deficiencies, and evaluating the adequacy of existing controls to mitigate identified risks. By aligning audit activities with risk priorities, organizations can focus on areas with the highest risk exposure and allocate resources efficiently to address control gaps and vulnerabilities. Additionally, continuous auditing methodologies enable organizations to automate audit processes and monitor controls in real-time to identify issues promptly and take corrective actions. Continuous auditing leverages technology-enabled audit tools and data analytics techniques to collect, analyze, and monitor audit-relevant data continuously. This approach enables auditors to identify trends, anomalies, and potential risks proactively and provide timely insights to management for decision-making and remediation. Furthermore, organizations may adopt integrated audit methodologies that combine multiple audit disciplines, such as IT audits, financial audits, and operational audits, to provide a holistic assessment of governance, risk, and compliance (GRC) practices. Integrated audit methodologies facilitate collaboration between different audit functions, streamline audit processes, and enhance the effectiveness of risk management and compliance efforts. Additionally, organizations may utilize agile audit methodologies to adapt audit processes and procedures dynamically to changing business environments, emerging risks, and regulatory requirements. Agile audit methodologies emphasize flexibility, collaboration, and iterative approaches to audit planning, execution, and reporting. By embracing agile principles, auditors can respond promptly to evolving risks and priorities, deliver value-added insights, and support organizational agility and resilience. In summary, audit methodologies play a critical role in evaluating governance and compliance practices, identifying control deficiencies, and mitigating risks effectively. By adopting structured audit approaches, leveraging technology-enabled audit tools, and embracing agile principles, organizations can enhance audit effectiveness, strengthen governance frameworks, and achieve compliance with regulatory requirements and industry standards. Assessing the effectiveness of governance controls is a crucial aspect of maintaining a robust governance framework and ensuring alignment with organizational objectives, regulatory requirements, and industry best practices. One commonly used approach for assessing governance controls is through conducting control self-assessments (CSAs), where individuals responsible for implementing and operating controls evaluate their effectiveness. CSAs involve evaluating control design adequacy and operational effectiveness based on predefined criteria and control objectives. Organizations may utilize standardized control assessment questionnaires or templates to facilitate the CSA process and ensure consistency across assessments. Additionally, organizations may employ control testing methodologies to validate control effectiveness and detect deficiencies. Control testing involves performing substantive tests, walkthroughs, and compliance reviews to assess control design and operating effectiveness. For example, in the context of information security governance, organizations may conduct penetration testing to assess the effectiveness of technical controls, such as firewalls, intrusion detection systems, and encryption mechanisms. Penetration testing involves simulating real-world cyber attacks to identify vulnerabilities and assess the organization's ability to prevent, detect, and respond to security incidents. Moreover, organizations may conduct control effectiveness reviews as part of internal audits or compliance assessments. Internal auditors evaluate the design and operating effectiveness of governance controls based on audit objectives, criteria, and risk assessments. Internal audit procedures may include reviewing control documentation, conducting interviews with control owners and stakeholders, and performing tests of controls to assess adherence to policies, procedures, and regulatory requirements. Furthermore, organizations may leverage key performance indicators (KPIs) and key risk indicators (KRIs) to monitor the effectiveness of governance controls continuously. KPIs measure the performance of governance processes and control activities, while KRIs provide early warning signals of potential risks and control deficiencies. By monitoring KPIs and KRIs, organizations can identify trends, anomalies, and emerging risks that may impact control effectiveness and take proactive measures to address them. Additionally, organizations may use control maturity models to assess the maturity level of governance controls and identify opportunities for improvement. Control maturity models, such as the Capability Maturity Model Integration (CMMI) framework, provide a structured approach for evaluating control maturity across different domains, including governance, risk management, and compliance. Organizations can use maturity assessments to benchmark their control maturity against industry standards and best practices, prioritize improvement initiatives, and track progress over time. Furthermore, organizations may leverage technology-enabled solutions, such as governance, risk, and compliance (GRC) platforms, to streamline control assessments, automate control testing processes, and centralize control monitoring activities. GRC platforms provide functionalities for documenting control frameworks, defining control objectives and requirements, conducting assessments, and generating reports and dashboards for monitoring control effectiveness. By implementing GRC solutions, organizations can enhance visibility into control performance, improve collaboration among stakeholders, and facilitate decision-making related to governance and risk management. Additionally, organizations may conduct control effectiveness benchmarking studies to compare their control performance against industry peers and identify leading practices and areas for improvement. Control effectiveness benchmarking involves collecting and analyzing data on control performance metrics, such as control testing results, control deficiencies, and compliance violations, and benchmarking them against industry benchmarks and standards. Through benchmarking exercises, organizations can gain insights into control effectiveness trends, identify gaps in control performance, and implement remediation measures to enhance governance control effectiveness. In summary, assessing the effectiveness of governance controls is essential for ensuring the integrity, reliability, and security of organizational operations and data. By leveraging various assessment approaches, including CSAs, control testing methodologies, internal audits, KPIs, KRIs, maturity models, technology solutions, and benchmarking studies, organizations can evaluate control effectiveness comprehensively, identify areas for improvement, and strengthen their governance frameworks to mitigate risks effectively.

Chapter 8: Continuous Monitoring and Improvement Strategies

Continuous monitoring plays a pivotal role in governance frameworks by providing real-time visibility into organizational processes, controls, and risks, thereby enhancing decision-making and risk management capabilities. With the ever-evolving threat landscape and regulatory requirements, organizations must adopt a proactive approach to monitoring to detect anomalies, deviations, and emerging risks promptly. Continuous monitoring encompasses various activities, including real-time data collection, analysis, and reporting, to assess the effectiveness of governance controls and ensure compliance with internal policies and external regulations. One of the key benefits of continuous monitoring is its ability to detect and respond to security incidents and compliance violations in a timely manner, minimizing the potential impact on the organization's operations and reputation. By leveraging automated monitoring tools and technologies, organizations can streamline the monitoring process and gain insights into control performance and compliance status across multiple dimensions. For instance, security information and event management (SIEM) solutions enable organizations to collect, correlate, and analyze security event data from various sources, such as network devices, servers, and applications, to detect suspicious activities and potential security breaches. Additionally, organizations can utilize log management and auditing tools to track user activities, system changes, and access permissions to identify unauthorized or suspicious behavior. Moreover, continuous monitoring allows organizations to proactively identify and address control deficiencies, process inefficiencies, and emerging risks before they escalate into significant issues. By monitoring key performance indicators (KPIs) and key risk indicators (KRIs), organizations can track the effectiveness of governance controls and identify areas for improvement. For example, organizations can monitor KPIs related to control performance, such as incident response times, patching compliance rates, and user access reviews, to measure the effectiveness of security controls and compliance activities. Similarly, organizations can track KRIs, such as the number of security incidents, frequency of compliance violations, and trend analysis of control deficiencies, to assess the overall risk posture and prioritize risk mitigation efforts. Additionally, continuous monitoring enables organizations to demonstrate compliance with regulatory requirements and industry standards by providing evidence of control effectiveness and adherence to predefined policies and procedures.

For instance, organizations subject to regulatory mandates, such as the Payment Card Industry Data Security Standard (PCI DSS) or the Health Insurance Portability and Accountability Act (HIPAA), must regularly monitor and audit their systems and processes to ensure compliance with data protection requirements. Continuous monitoring also supports governance initiatives, such as internal audits, risk assessments, and compliance reviews, by providing auditors and stakeholders with timely and accurate information to assess control effectiveness and compliance status. Furthermore, continuous monitoring fosters a culture of accountability, transparency, and continuous improvement within the organization by promoting collaboration and communication among stakeholders. By providing stakeholders with access to real-time monitoring dashboards, reports, and alerts, organizations can enhance awareness of governance issues and facilitate timely decision-making and remediation actions. Additionally, continuous monitoring enables organizations to adapt quickly to changing business environments, emerging threats, and regulatory changes by adjusting monitoring strategies and control frameworks accordingly. For instance, organizations can enhance monitoring capabilities in response to new cyber threats or compliance requirements by deploying additional sensors, implementing new monitoring policies, or enhancing data analytics capabilities. In summary, continuous monitoring is essential for effective governance by providing organizations with real-time visibility into control performance, compliance status, and emerging risks. By leveraging automated monitoring tools, tracking KPIs and KRIs, demonstrating compliance, supporting governance initiatives, fostering collaboration, and adapting to changes, organizations can enhance their governance capabilities and mitigate risks proactively. Continuous improvement is a fundamental aspect of governance frameworks, as it ensures that organizations adapt to evolving business environments, technological advancements, and regulatory requirements. By implementing strategies for continuous improvement, organizations can enhance the effectiveness, efficiency, and agility of their governance processes, thereby driving better outcomes and mitigating risks. One strategy for continuous improvement is to establish a structured framework for governance that incorporates feedback mechanisms, performance metrics, and regular reviews to identify areas for enhancement. For example, organizations can adopt the Plan-Do-Check-Act (PDCA) cycle, also known as the Deming cycle, to systematically plan, implement, monitor, and refine governance activities. The PDCA cycle involves four key stages: Plan, where goals, objectives, and strategies are defined; Do, where the planned activities are executed; Check, where performance is monitored, measured, and evaluated against predefined metrics; and Act, where adjustments and improvements are made based on the evaluation results. By following the PDCA cycle, organizations can iteratively improve their governance processes and achieve better outcomes over time. Another strategy for continuous improvement is to leverage technology and automation to streamline governance activities, increase efficiency, and reduce manual effort. For example, organizations can implement governance, risk, and compliance (GRC) software solutions to automate the collection, analysis, and reporting of governance data, thereby saving time and resources. Additionally, organizations can utilize robotic process automation (RPA) tools to automate repetitive tasks, such as data entry, validation, and reconciliation, freeing up staff to focus on more value-added activities. By embracing technology and automation, organizations can accelerate governance processes, improve data accuracy, and enhance decision-making capabilities. Furthermore, organizations can foster a culture of innovation and learning by encouraging collaboration, knowledge sharing, and continuous professional development among employees. For instance, organizations can establish cross-functional teams or communities of practice to facilitate collaboration and knowledge exchange among governance professionals from different departments or business units. Additionally, organizations can provide training, workshops, and certifications to employees to enhance their skills, competencies, and understanding of governance principles and best practices. By investing in employee development and empowerment, organizations can build a capable and resilient workforce that drives continuous improvement in governance. Moreover, organizations can enhance their governance practices by actively seeking feedback from stakeholders, including employees, customers, partners, and regulators. For example, organizations can conduct surveys, interviews, and focus groups to gather feedback on governance processes, controls, and performance. Additionally, organizations can establish governance committees or advisory boards comprising internal and external stakeholders to provide guidance, oversight, and feedback on governance initiatives. By soliciting and incorporating feedback from stakeholders, organizations can identify blind spots, gaps, and opportunities for improvement in their governance practices. In summary, continuous improvement is essential for effective governance as it enables organizations to adapt, innovate, and excel in a dynamic and complex business environment. By implementing strategies such as establishing structured frameworks, leveraging technology and automation, fostering a culture of innovation, learning and seeking feedback from stakeholders, organizations can drive continuous improvement in governance and achieve better outcomes.

Chapter 9: Managing Third-Party and Vendor Compliance

Vendor management plays a crucial role in governance and compliance frameworks, as organizations increasingly rely on third-party vendors and suppliers to support their operations, deliver services, and manage critical functions. Effective vendor management ensures that organizations can mitigate risks, maintain regulatory compliance, and uphold security standards throughout the vendor lifecycle. One key aspect of vendor management is the vendor assessment process, where organizations evaluate potential vendors based on their capabilities, reputation, financial stability, and adherence to compliance requirements. This process involves gathering information about vendors, such as their business practices, security controls, and certifications, to assess their suitability and reliability. To conduct vendor assessments, organizations can use various tools and techniques, including vendor questionnaires, risk assessments, and due diligence reviews. For example, organizations can develop standardized vendor assessment questionnaires to collect relevant information about vendors' security practices, data handling processes, and regulatory compliance. Additionally, organizations can perform risk assessments to identify and prioritize potential risks associated with vendor relationships, such as data breaches, service disruptions, or compliance violations. These assessments help organizations make informed decisions about whether to engage with specific vendors and what risk mitigation measures are necessary. Once vendors are onboarded, organizations must establish clear contractual agreements and service-level agreements (SLAs) to define expectations, responsibilities, and performance metrics. Contracts should address key areas such as data protection, confidentiality, compliance requirements, indemnification, and termination clauses. SLAs should specify service levels, uptime guarantees, response times, and escalation procedures to ensure that vendors meet agreed-upon performance standards. To monitor vendor compliance and performance, organizations should implement ongoing oversight and monitoring mechanisms. This includes regular reviews of vendor performance against contractual obligations and SLAs, as well as periodic audits and assessments to validate compliance with regulatory requirements and industry standards. Organizations can leverage technology solutions, such as vendor management software or GRC platforms, to automate vendor monitoring processes and streamline communication with vendors.

Additionally, organizations should establish robust incident response and escalation procedures to address any issues or breaches involving vendors promptly. This includes defining roles and responsibilities, establishing communication channels, and coordinating responses with relevant stakeholders, including legal, compliance, and IT teams. In the event of a vendor-related incident, organizations should conduct thorough investigations to identify root causes, assess impacts, and implement corrective actions to prevent recurrence. Furthermore, vendor management should be an integral part of the overall risk management framework, with vendors considered as potential sources of risk that need to be identified, assessed, and managed accordingly. This involves integrating vendor risk assessments into the organization's broader risk management processes, such as risk identification, analysis, and mitigation. By adopting a proactive and comprehensive approach to vendor management, organizations can minimize risks, ensure regulatory compliance, and safeguard their reputation and brand integrity. This includes ongoing monitoring of vendor relationships, regular reassessment of vendor risks, and continuous improvement of vendor management practices to adapt to changing business and regulatory landscapes. In summary, effective vendor management is essential for organizations to navigate the complexities of the modern business environment while maintaining compliance with regulatory requirements and industry standards. By implementing robust vendor assessment processes, clear contractual agreements, proactive monitoring mechanisms, and integrated risk management practices, organizations can mitigate risks associated with vendor relationships and foster trust, transparency, and accountability throughout the vendor lifecycle. Ensuring third-party compliance with governance standards is paramount for organizations to maintain trust, security, and regulatory adherence in their business ecosystem. One crucial aspect of this process involves establishing clear expectations and requirements for third-party vendors and partners. Organizations must define their governance standards and communicate these expectations effectively to their third-party stakeholders. This can include outlining specific compliance frameworks, security protocols, data protection measures, and ethical guidelines that vendors are expected to follow. To facilitate this communication, organizations can leverage various channels, such as vendor contracts, policies, training sessions, and regular meetings to ensure alignment and understanding of governance standards. Additionally, organizations should conduct thorough due diligence when selecting third-party vendors to assess their compliance posture and ensure alignment with organizational standards. This due diligence process may involve reviewing vendors' compliance documentation, certifications, audit reports, and security controls to verify their adherence to relevant governance standards. For example, organizations can request vendors to provide evidence of compliance with industry-specific regulations, such as GDPR, HIPAA, or PCI DSS, depending on the nature of the services provided and the data involved. Furthermore, organizations should incorporate vendor compliance assessments into their overall risk management framework to identify and mitigate potential risks associated with third-party relationships. This involves evaluating vendors' risk profiles, assessing their impact on organizational objectives, and implementing appropriate risk mitigation strategies. Organizations can utilize risk assessment methodologies, such as risk matrices, risk registers, and risk scoring models, to prioritize and address vendor-related risks effectively. Once vendors are onboarded, organizations should establish robust monitoring and oversight mechanisms to ensure ongoing compliance with governance standards. This includes regular performance reviews, audits, and assessments to evaluate vendors' adherence to contractual obligations, regulatory requirements, and industry best practices. Organizations can use technology solutions, such as vendor management software or GRC platforms, to automate and streamline the monitoring process, track compliance metrics, and generate reports for stakeholders. Additionally, organizations should conduct periodic reviews and updates of their governance standards to reflect changes in regulations, industry trends, and emerging risks. This ensures that governance requirements remain relevant and effective in addressing evolving threats and challenges. Furthermore, organizations should foster a culture of compliance and accountability among third-party vendors by providing ongoing training, guidance, and support. This can include offering educational resources, conducting awareness sessions, and establishing channels for vendors to report compliance issues or seek clarification on governance standards. By promoting a collaborative and proactive approach to compliance, organizations can strengthen their relationships with third-party vendors and enhance overall governance effectiveness. In summary, ensuring third-party compliance with governance standards is essential for organizations to mitigate risks, maintain regulatory compliance, and safeguard their reputation and brand integrity. By establishing clear expectations, conducting thorough due diligence, integrating compliance assessments into risk management processes, implementing robust monitoring mechanisms, and fostering a culture of compliance, organizations can effectively manage third-party relationships and uphold governance standards across their business ecosystem.

Chapter 10: Governance and Compliance Challenges in Emerging Technologies

Addressing governance gaps in emerging technologies is imperative for organizations to adapt to the evolving digital landscape and effectively manage associated risks. One significant challenge organizations face is the rapid pace of technological advancements, which often outpaces the development of governance frameworks and regulatory guidelines. To bridge these gaps, organizations must adopt proactive measures to identify, assess, and address governance gaps in emerging technologies. One approach is to establish cross-functional teams comprising experts from various disciplines, including IT, legal, compliance, and risk management, to collaboratively assess the impact of emerging technologies on governance frameworks. These teams can conduct comprehensive risk assessments to identify potential gaps in existing governance structures and develop strategies to mitigate associated risks. Additionally, organizations should stay abreast of emerging technologies and their potential implications for governance by actively monitoring industry trends, attending relevant conferences, and participating in professional networks. By gaining insights into emerging technologies early on, organizations can proactively update their governance frameworks to address potential gaps and ensure alignment with industry best practices and regulatory requirements. Furthermore, organizations should leverage automation and technology solutions to enhance governance effectiveness in managing emerging technology risks. For example, organizations can deploy advanced analytics tools to monitor data flows, detect anomalies, and identify potential compliance violations in real-time. Similarly, organizations can implement blockchain technology to enhance transparency, traceability, and accountability in supply chain management, financial transactions, and data sharing processes. Moreover, organizations should prioritize cybersecurity measures to protect against emerging threats associated with new technologies. This includes implementing robust access controls, encryption protocols, and intrusion detection systems to safeguard critical assets and sensitive information from unauthorized access and cyberattacks. Additionally, organizations should conduct regular security audits and penetration testing to identify vulnerabilities and address security gaps proactively. Furthermore, organizations should ensure that their governance frameworks are adaptable and agile enough to accommodate the rapid changes brought about by emerging technologies. This involves establishing flexible policies and procedures that can evolve in response to new threats, vulnerabilities, and regulatory requirements. Additionally, organizations should foster a culture of innovation and experimentation to encourage employees to explore and leverage emerging technologies responsibly. This can include providing training and professional development opportunities to equip employees with the knowledge and skills needed to navigate the complexities of emerging technologies and make informed governance decisions. Furthermore, organizations should collaborate with industry peers, regulatory bodies, and standards-setting organizations to develop consensus-based approaches to addressing governance gaps in emerging technologies. By sharing insights, best practices, and lessons learned, organizations can collectively enhance governance effectiveness and mitigate risks associated with emerging technologies. In summary, addressing governance gaps in emerging technologies requires a proactive and multidisciplinary approach that combines technological expertise, regulatory compliance, risk management, and cybersecurity measures. By establishing cross-functional teams, staying abreast of industry trends, leveraging automation and technology solutions, prioritizing cybersecurity measures, fostering a culture of innovation, and collaborating with stakeholders, organizations can effectively manage the risks and opportunities presented by emerging technologies and ensure alignment with governance objectives. Compliance considerations for cutting-edge technologies are crucial for organizations seeking to leverage innovative solutions while maintaining regulatory adherence and mitigating associated risks. One significant challenge in adopting cutting-edge technologies is ensuring compliance with existing regulations, which may not have provisions specifically addressing these novel advancements. To address this challenge, organizations must conduct thorough assessments of regulatory requirements and industry standards relevant to the specific technologies being implemented. For example, in deploying artificial intelligence (AI) systems for automated decision-making processes, organizations must ensure compliance with data protection regulations such as the General Data Protection Regulation (GDPR) by implementing mechanisms for data transparency, accountability, and user consent. Similarly, organizations adopting blockchain technology must navigate regulatory landscapes related to data privacy, cybersecurity, and financial transactions, ensuring compliance with laws such as the European Union's Anti-Money Laundering Directive and the Securities and Exchange Commission's regulations on digital assets. Moreover, organizations should establish clear governance frameworks and policies governing the responsible use of cutting-edge technologies to ensure alignment with regulatory requirements and ethical standards. This includes developing guidelines for data collection, processing, and storage, as well as mechanisms for addressing ethical concerns such as bias, fairness, and accountability in AI algorithms. Additionally, organizations should implement robust security measures to safeguard sensitive data and intellectual property associated with cutting-edge technologies. This may involve deploying encryption protocols, access controls, and secure authentication mechanisms to protect against unauthorized access, data breaches, and cyber threats. Furthermore, organizations should prioritize ongoing monitoring and assessment of compliance risks associated with cutting-edge technologies to identify emerging regulatory trends, updates, and enforcement actions. This includes conducting regular audits, assessments, and impact analyses to ensure that technology deployments remain compliant with evolving regulatory requirements and industry standards. Additionally, organizations should foster a culture of compliance awareness and accountability across all levels of the organization by providing training, education, and resources to employees on regulatory requirements and ethical considerations related to cutting-edge technologies. This can help mitigate the risk of non-compliance and ensure that employees understand their roles and responsibilities in upholding legal and ethical standards. Moreover, organizations should engage in proactive collaboration and dialogue with regulatory authorities, industry associations, and other stakeholders to stay informed about regulatory developments and seek guidance on compliance matters related to cutting-edge technologies. By actively participating in industry forums, working groups, and regulatory consultations, organizations can influence policy discussions, shape regulatory frameworks, and advocate for practical solutions that balance innovation with regulatory compliance. Additionally, organizations should leverage technology solutions and automation tools to streamline compliance processes, enhance transparency, and demonstrate adherence to regulatory requirements. This may include implementing compliance management software, risk assessment tools, and audit tracking systems to facilitate compliance monitoring, reporting, and documentation. Furthermore, organizations should conduct regular risk assessments and scenario analyses to identify potential compliance gaps, vulnerabilities, and areas for improvement in their use of cutting-edge technologies. This proactive approach can help organizations anticipate regulatory challenges, address emerging risks, and implement effective controls to maintain compliance while maximizing the benefits of innovative technologies. In summary, compliance considerations for cutting-edge technologies require a proactive and holistic approach that encompasses legal, ethical, and operational dimensions. By understanding regulatory requirements, establishing clear governance frameworks, implementing robust security measures, fostering a culture of compliance, engaging with stakeholders, leveraging technology solutions, and conducting regular risk assessments, organizations can navigate the complex regulatory landscape and ensure compliance while driving innovation and growth.

BOOK 4
EXPERT TECHNIQUES FOR INCIDENT RESPONSE
AND DISASTER RECOVERY IN CISM

ROB BOTWRIGHT

Chapter 1: Foundations of Incident Response and Disaster Recovery

Principles of incident response are fundamental guidelines and strategies designed to effectively manage and mitigate cybersecurity incidents within an organization's information technology infrastructure. These principles encompass various stages of incident response, including preparation, detection, containment, eradication, recovery, and lessons learned. One of the core principles of incident response is preparedness, which involves establishing proactive measures and protocols to detect, respond to, and recover from security incidents. This includes developing incident response plans, defining roles and responsibilities, and conducting regular training and exercises to ensure readiness. Incident response plans outline the steps to be taken in the event of a security incident, including communication procedures, escalation paths, and coordination with internal and external stakeholders. These plans should be regularly reviewed, updated, and tested to address evolving threats and organizational changes. Another key principle of incident response is rapid detection, which involves identifying and assessing security incidents as soon as possible to minimize their impact. This may involve deploying security monitoring tools and technologies to monitor network traffic, log files, and system activity for signs of unauthorized access, malware infections, or other suspicious behavior. Security information and event management (SIEM) systems, intrusion detection systems (IDS), and endpoint detection and response (EDR) solutions are commonly used to automate the detection and analysis of security incidents. Once a security incident is detected, the principle of containment comes into play, aiming to prevent the incident from spreading further and causing additional damage. This may involve isolating affected systems, disabling compromised accounts, and blocking malicious traffic to contain the scope of the incident. Network segmentation, firewall rules, and access controls can help limit the spread of malware and unauthorized access within the organization's infrastructure. Following containment, the next principle is eradication, which involves removing the root cause of the security incident and restoring affected systems to a secure state. This may require identifying and removing malware, patching vulnerabilities, and restoring data from backups to mitigate the impact of the incident. Incident responders may use various tools and techniques, such as antivirus software, malware analysis tools, and forensic investigation methods, to identify and remediate security vulnerabilities and threats. Once the incident has been contained and eradicated, the focus shifts to recovery, which involves restoring normal operations and minimizing the impact on business operations. This may include restoring data from backups, rebuilding affected systems, and implementing additional security controls to prevent similar incidents from occurring in the future. Disaster recovery plans and business continuity plans play a crucial role in ensuring the timely recovery of critical systems and services following a security incident. Finally, the principle of lessons learned emphasizes the importance of conducting post-incident reviews and analysis to identify root causes, vulnerabilities, and areas for improvement in the organization's incident response capabilities. This may involve documenting lessons learned, updating incident response plans, and implementing corrective actions to enhance the organization's resilience to future security incidents. By applying these principles of incident response, organizations can effectively detect, contain, and recover from security incidents while minimizing their impact on business operations and reputation. Understanding disaster recovery fundamentals is essential for organizations to ensure the resilience of their operations in the face of unforeseen events that could disrupt business continuity. Disaster recovery refers to the process of restoring IT infrastructure, systems, and data following a disruptive event, such as natural disasters, cyberattacks, or hardware failures. At its core, disaster recovery aims to minimize downtime, mitigate data loss, and restore normal operations as quickly as possible. One fundamental aspect of disaster recovery is risk assessment, which involves identifying potential threats and vulnerabilities that could impact the organization's IT infrastructure and data. This may include conducting a business impact analysis (BIA) to assess the potential consequences of different disaster scenarios and prioritize recovery efforts based on their criticality to the business. Another key fundamental of disaster recovery is planning, which involves developing comprehensive plans and procedures to guide the organization's response to a disaster. This includes defining roles and responsibilities, establishing communication protocols, and outlining the steps to be taken to recover IT systems and data. Disaster recovery plans should be regularly tested and updated to ensure their effectiveness in real-world scenarios. One commonly used technique for disaster recovery planning is the creation of backup and recovery strategies, which involve making copies of critical data and storing them in secure locations. This may include implementing backup solutions such as tape backups, disk backups, or cloud-based backups to ensure data redundancy and availability in the event of a disaster. Backup and recovery solutions should be configured to meet the organization's recovery time objectives (RTOs) and recovery point objectives (RPOs), which define the acceptable amount of downtime and data loss in the event of a disaster. In addition to backup and recovery, organizations should also consider implementing high availability and failover mechanisms to minimize downtime and ensure continuous access to critical services. This may include deploying redundant hardware, clustering servers, or leveraging virtualization technologies to facilitate rapid failover and recovery in the event of a hardware or software failure. Disaster recovery planning should also address the human aspect of disaster response, including training employees on their roles and responsibilities during a disaster and conducting regular drills and exercises to ensure readiness. This may involve simulating different disaster scenarios, such as network outages, data breaches, or natural disasters, and evaluating the organization's response and recovery capabilities. Furthermore, organizations should establish partnerships with external vendors, service providers, and other stakeholders to ensure access to additional resources and expertise during a disaster. This may include contracting with disaster recovery service providers, cloud service providers, or colocation facilities to facilitate offsite data storage, backup, and recovery. Additionally, organizations should consider the regulatory and compliance requirements that may impact their disaster recovery planning and implementation efforts. This may include industry-specific regulations, such as HIPAA for healthcare organizations or PCI DSS for payment card industry compliance, which mandate specific data protection and recovery measures. By understanding these fundamental principles of disaster recovery and implementing robust planning, preparation, and response measures, organizations can enhance their resilience and minimize the impact of disruptive events on their operations and reputation.

Chapter 2: Incident Response Planning and Preparedness

Developing incident response plans is a critical aspect of cybersecurity preparedness for organizations aiming to effectively mitigate and manage security incidents. Incident response plans serve as comprehensive guides outlining the steps and procedures to be followed in the event of a security breach, cyberattack, or any other form of security incident. One key aspect of developing incident response plans is conducting a thorough risk assessment to identify potential security threats and vulnerabilities that could impact the organization's IT infrastructure and data. This may involve evaluating the organization's network architecture, systems, applications, and data repositories to identify potential attack vectors and weak points. Once the risks have been identified, organizations can develop incident response plans tailored to address specific types of security incidents and their potential impact on the business. This includes defining roles and responsibilities for different stakeholders within the organization, such as incident response team members, IT staff, legal counsel, and senior management. Incident response plans should also outline the communication protocols to be followed during a security incident, including how and when to notify relevant stakeholders, such as employees, customers, partners, regulators, and law enforcement agencies. This may involve establishing communication channels such as email, phone, or incident response platforms to ensure timely and effective communication. In addition to defining roles and responsibilities, incident response plans should also include detailed procedures for detecting, analyzing, and containing security incidents. This may involve implementing security controls and monitoring mechanisms to detect suspicious activities or anomalies in the organization's IT environment. Once a security incident has been detected, organizations should have procedures in place to contain the incident and prevent further damage or unauthorized access to systems and data. This may include isolating affected systems, disabling compromised user accounts, or blocking malicious IP addresses at the network level. Incident response plans should also include procedures for investigating security incidents to determine the root cause, extent of the damage, and any data breaches that may have occurred. This may involve conducting forensic analysis of affected systems and logs to identify the source of the attack and the data accessed or compromised by the attacker. Once the incident has been contained and investigated, organizations should have procedures in place for remediation and recovery. This may involve restoring affected systems and data from backups, patching security vulnerabilities, and implementing additional security controls to prevent similar incidents from occurring in the future. Organizations should also have procedures in place for documenting and reporting security incidents to relevant stakeholders, such as regulatory authorities, customers, and business partners. This may involve maintaining detailed incident logs, conducting post-incident reviews, and preparing incident reports summarizing the incident, its impact, and the organization's response. Finally, incident response plans should be regularly tested, reviewed, and updated to ensure their effectiveness in real-world scenarios. This may involve conducting tabletop exercises, simulated attack scenarios, or red team exercises to evaluate the organization's readiness and response capabilities. By developing and maintaining robust incident response plans, organizations can effectively mitigate security risks, minimize the impact of security incidents, and maintain the trust and confidence of their stakeholders. Preparedness measures for incident response are essential components of any organization's cybersecurity strategy, ensuring readiness to effectively detect, respond to, and recover from security incidents. One crucial aspect of preparedness is the establishment of an incident response team comprising individuals with specialized skills and expertise in cybersecurity, forensics, legal, and communications. This team is responsible for orchestrating the organization's response to security incidents, coordinating activities, and ensuring a timely and effective response. To facilitate communication and collaboration among team members, organizations often deploy collaboration tools such as Slack or Microsoft Teams. These platforms enable team members to communicate in real-time, share information, and coordinate response efforts more efficiently. Additionally, organizations establish incident response policies and procedures that outline the roles, responsibilities, and processes to be followed during a security incident. These policies should be well-documented, regularly reviewed, and communicated to all relevant stakeholders to ensure clarity and consistency in the response process. Incident response policies often include predefined escalation paths for reporting and responding to security incidents based on their severity and impact on the organization. For example, in the event of a data breach, the incident response policy may specify that the incident response team must be immediately notified, followed by the legal department and senior management. Moreover, organizations conduct regular training and awareness programs to educate employees about their roles and responsibilities in responding to security incidents. This training covers topics such as recognizing common security threats, reporting suspicious activities, and following incident response procedures. Through interactive workshops, simulations, and scenario-based training exercises, employees are better equipped to identify and respond to security incidents effectively. Furthermore, organizations implement technical controls and monitoring solutions to enhance their ability to detect and respond to security incidents proactively. This includes deploying intrusion detection systems (IDS), intrusion prevention systems (IPS), security information and event management (SIEM) solutions, and endpoint detection and response (EDR) tools. These tools help organizations monitor network traffic, identify anomalous behavior, and detect signs of potential security breaches in real-time. In addition to technical controls, organizations conduct regular vulnerability assessments and penetration testing to identify and remediate security weaknesses before they can be exploited by attackers. Vulnerability scanners such as Nessus or OpenVAS are commonly used to scan networks, systems, and applications for known vulnerabilities and misconfigurations. Penetration testing, on the other hand, involves simulating real-world attacks to identify potential entry points and assess the effectiveness of existing security controls. By identifying and addressing vulnerabilities proactively, organizations can reduce their risk exposure and strengthen their overall security posture. Furthermore, organizations establish relationships with external partners, such as incident response service providers, law enforcement agencies, and industry groups, to enhance their incident response capabilities. These partnerships enable organizations to leverage external expertise, resources, and support during security incidents, such as forensic investigation services or legal assistance. Additionally, organizations establish incident response playbooks that document step-by-step procedures for responding to specific types of security incidents. These playbooks include predefined workflows, checklists, and response templates to guide incident responders through the response process systematically. By following these playbooks, organizations can ensure consistency and efficiency in their response efforts, even during high-stress situations. Moreover, organizations conduct regular tabletop exercises and simulations to test their incident response plans and procedures in a controlled environment. These exercises simulate various security scenarios, such as ransomware attacks, data breaches, or DDoS attacks, and allow the incident response team to practice their response strategies and communication protocols. Through these exercises, organizations can identify gaps in their incident response plans, refine their procedures, and improve their overall readiness to respond to security incidents effectively. Additionally, organizations establish relationships with external partners, such as incident response service providers, law enforcement agencies, and industry groups, to enhance their incident response capabilities. These partnerships enable organizations to leverage external expertise, resources, and support during security incidents, such as forensic investigation services or legal assistance. Additionally, organizations establish relationships with external partners, such as incident response service providers, law enforcement agencies, and industry groups, to enhance their incident response capabilities. These partnerships enable organizations to leverage external expertise, resources, and support during security incidents, such as forensic investigation services or legal assistance.

Chapter 3: Incident Detection and Analysis Techniques

Methods for detecting incidents play a crucial role in the overall security posture of an organization, providing the means to identify unauthorized access, malicious activities, or suspicious behavior within the network or system environment. One commonly used method for detecting incidents is through the implementation of intrusion detection systems (IDS) and intrusion prevention systems (IPS). These systems continuously monitor network traffic and analyze it for signs of potential security threats or anomalies. Snort is a popular open-source IDS/IPS tool that can be deployed on a network to detect and prevent various types of attacks, such as network reconnaissance, malware infections, or denial-of-service (DoS) attacks. Another method for detecting incidents is through the use of security information and event management (SIEM) solutions. SIEM tools collect, aggregate, and analyze log data from various sources, such as servers, firewalls, and endpoint devices, to identify security incidents or suspicious activities. Splunk is a widely used SIEM solution that can correlate data from multiple sources to detect security threats and anomalies effectively. Additionally, organizations can deploy endpoint detection and response (EDR) solutions to detect and respond to security incidents on individual endpoints, such as desktops, laptops, or servers. CrowdStrike Falcon is a leading EDR platform that provides real-time visibility into endpoint activities and enables organizations to detect and remediate threats quickly. Furthermore, organizations can leverage threat intelligence feeds to enhance their incident detection capabilities. Threat intelligence feeds provide information about known threats, vulnerabilities, and malicious actors, allowing organizations to proactively identify and block potential security threats before they can cause harm. Open-source threat intelligence platforms like MISP (Malware Information Sharing Platform) enable organizations to aggregate, share, and analyze threat intelligence data from various sources to improve their incident detection and response capabilities. Additionally, organizations can use network traffic analysis tools to monitor and analyze network traffic for signs of suspicious or malicious activities. Wireshark is a popular open-source network protocol analyzer that allows security analysts to capture and inspect network packets in real-time, helping them identify abnormal behavior or potential security threats. Moreover, organizations can implement file integrity monitoring (FIM) solutions to detect unauthorized changes to critical system files or configurations. FIM tools monitor file systems for any modifications and alert administrators when changes are detected, helping them identify and respond to potential security incidents promptly. OSSEC (Open Source Security) is a widely used FIM tool that can monitor file integrity, log files, registry entries, and other system attributes for signs of compromise. Additionally, organizations can deploy honeypots as a proactive measure to detect and analyze potential security threats. Honeypots are decoy systems or services designed to attract and lure attackers, allowing organizations to gather information about their tactics, techniques, and procedures (TTPs). Tools like Honeyd enable organizations to deploy and manage honeypots effectively, helping them gain valuable insights into emerging threats and attack patterns. Moreover, organizations can implement user and entity behavior analytics (UEBA) solutions to detect abnormal behavior or activities that may indicate a security incident. UEBA tools analyze user and entity behavior patterns to identify deviations from normal behavior and alert security teams to potential security risks or threats. Exabeam is a leading UEBA platform that uses machine learning and advanced analytics to detect insider threats, account compromises, and other security incidents proactively. Additionally, organizations can leverage cloud-based security services and platforms to enhance their incident detection capabilities. Cloud-based security solutions, such as Cloud Access Security Brokers (CASBs) or cloud-native security services, provide real-time visibility and control over cloud environments, enabling organizations to detect and respond to security incidents across their cloud infrastructure. Overall, by leveraging a combination of these methods and technologies, organizations can enhance their ability to detect and respond to security incidents effectively, reducing the risk of data breaches, financial losses, and reputational damage. Incident analysis is a critical process in incident response that involves examining the details and characteristics of security incidents to understand their nature, scope, and impact. One commonly used technique for incident analysis is log analysis, which involves reviewing system logs, network traffic logs, and application logs to identify relevant events and activities leading up to the incident. Log files can contain valuable information about user actions, system events, and network connections, helping analysts reconstruct the timeline of an incident and identify the root cause. The `grep` command is often used in the command line interface (CLI) to search through log files for specific keywords or patterns. For example, `grep "ERROR" logfile.txt` can be used to search for error messages in a log file. Another technique for incident analysis is memory forensics, which involves analyzing the volatile memory (RAM) of compromised systems to extract information about running processes, network connections, and malicious code injections. Tools like Volatility Framework provide a set of command-line tools for analyzing memory dumps obtained from compromised systems. Analysts can use commands like `volatility pslist` to list running processes or `volatility netscan` to scan for network connections in memory dumps. Additionally, disk forensics is another essential technique for incident analysis, which involves examining the contents of disk images or hard drives to identify evidence of unauthorized access, malware infections, or data exfiltration. The `dd` command is commonly used to create disk images, which can then be analyzed using forensic tools like The Sleuth Kit (TSK) or Autopsy. Analysts can use commands like `dd if=/dev/sda of=image.dd` to create a disk image of a compromised system's hard drive. Network traffic analysis is another valuable technique for incident analysis, which involves capturing and analyzing network packets to identify malicious activities or communication with known command-and-control (C2) servers. Tools like Wireshark provide a graphical user interface (GUI) for analyzing network traffic, but analysts can also use command-line tools like `tcpdump` to capture and analyze network packets. Additionally, behavioral analysis is an important technique for incident analysis, which involves observing and analyzing the behavior of malware or suspicious files in a controlled environment to understand their capabilities and impact. Sandboxing tools like Cuckoo Sandbox or hybrid-analysis.com provide environments for executing and analyzing suspicious files in a safe manner. Analysts can submit suspicious files to these platforms and analyze the behavior and actions taken by the files during execution. Furthermore, threat intelligence analysis is a crucial aspect of incident analysis, which involves correlating information about security threats, vulnerabilities, and indicators of compromise (IOCs) from various sources to identify patterns and trends associated with security incidents. Threat intelligence platforms like MISP or ThreatConnect provide capabilities for collecting, analyzing, and sharing threat intelligence data with other organizations and security professionals. Analysts can use these platforms to enrich their incident data with contextual information about known threats and attack patterns. Moreover, collaboration and information sharing among security teams and industry peers are essential for effective incident analysis. Platforms like Slack or Microsoft Teams provide communication and collaboration tools for security teams to share information, discuss findings, and coordinate response efforts in real-time. By leveraging these techniques and tools, security analysts can conduct thorough incident analysis to identify the root cause of security incidents, assess their impact, and develop effective response strategies to mitigate further risks and prevent future incidents.

Chapter 4: Incident Classification and Prioritization

Classifying incident severity levels is a crucial aspect of incident response, providing a framework for prioritizing and allocating resources based on the impact and urgency of each incident. One commonly used approach for classifying incident severity levels is the use of a predefined scale or matrix that categorizes incidents into different levels based on their impact on the organization's operations, data, and reputation. For example, a four-level severity scale may include categories such as low, medium, high, and critical, with each level representing a different degree of impact and urgency. Incident severity levels are typically determined based on several factors, including the potential impact on critical systems or data, the extent of disruption to business operations, the sensitivity of the information involved, and the potential regulatory or legal implications. In some cases, incident severity levels may also be influenced by external factors such as industry standards, regulatory requirements, or contractual obligations. When classifying incident severity levels, it's essential to consider the specific context and circumstances of each incident, as well as the organization's risk tolerance and business priorities. Incident severity levels are often defined in the organization's incident response policy or playbook, which provides guidance on how to assess and categorize incidents based on their severity. Once incidents are classified into different severity levels, appropriate response actions and escalation procedures can be implemented based on the severity level assigned to each incident. For example, low-severity incidents may require minimal intervention and can be handled by frontline support staff, while critical-severity incidents may require immediate attention from senior management and specialized response teams. Incident severity levels can also serve as a basis for prioritizing response efforts and resource allocation during incident response activities. For example, organizations may allocate more resources and prioritize response efforts for incidents classified as high or critical severity, while low-severity incidents may receive less immediate attention. Additionally, incident severity levels can help organizations track and report on the overall effectiveness of their incident response efforts, providing insights into trends and patterns related to incident frequency, impact, and resolution times. By consistently classifying incidents into different severity levels and applying appropriate response measures based on the severity level assigned to each incident, organizations can effectively manage and mitigate security risks, minimize the impact of incidents on their operations, and maintain the confidentiality, integrity, and availability of their information assets. Prioritizing incident response actions is a critical aspect of managing cybersecurity incidents effectively, ensuring that resources are allocated efficiently to mitigate the most significant risks promptly. One approach to prioritizing incident response actions is to use a risk-based approach, which involves assessing the potential impact and likelihood of each incident and prioritizing actions based on their risk level. To prioritize incident response actions using a risk-based approach, organizations can utilize risk assessment methodologies such as qualitative risk assessment, quantitative risk assessment, or a combination of both. Qualitative risk assessment involves evaluating the severity and likelihood of potential impacts associated with each incident based on subjective criteria such as expert judgment, historical data, and industry best practices. In contrast, quantitative risk assessment involves assigning numerical values to the severity and likelihood of potential impacts and using mathematical models to calculate the overall risk level. By assessing incidents based on their risk level, organizations can prioritize response actions accordingly, focusing on addressing high-risk incidents first to minimize their potential impact on the organization's operations, data, and reputation.

Another approach to prioritizing incident response actions is to consider the criticality of affected systems or assets. Organizations can classify systems and assets based on their importance to the organization's operations, with critical systems and assets receiving higher priority for incident response actions. For example, a cybersecurity incident that affects a mission-critical system or sensitive data repository may require immediate attention and prioritization of resources to minimize the impact on business operations and protect sensitive information. Additionally, organizations can prioritize incident response actions based on regulatory or legal requirements, contractual obligations, or industry standards. For example, incidents that involve potential data breaches or violations of privacy regulations may require immediate reporting to regulatory authorities and affected individuals, necessitating prioritization of response actions to ensure compliance with legal requirements. Furthermore, organizations can prioritize incident response actions based on the potential for reputational damage or harm to customer trust. Incidents that have the potential to tarnish the organization's reputation or erode customer confidence may require swift and decisive action to mitigate the reputational impact and restore trust. By prioritizing incident response actions based on factors such as risk level, criticality of affected systems or assets, regulatory and legal requirements, and reputational impact, organizations can effectively allocate resources and respond to cybersecurity incidents in a timely and efficient manner, minimizing the impact on their operations and stakeholders.

Chapter 5: Incident Containment and Eradication Strategies

Containment of cybersecurity incidents is crucial to prevent further damage and limit the impact on an organization's systems, data, and operations. One strategy for containing incidents is to isolate affected systems or networks to prevent the spread of malware or unauthorized access. This can be achieved by disconnecting compromised systems from the network or implementing network segmentation to restrict communication between infected and unaffected systems. For example, in the case of a ransomware attack, organizations can use network access control (NAC) or firewall rules to block communication between infected endpoints and other network resources. Another strategy for containing incidents is to implement access controls and privilege management to limit the actions that attackers can perform on compromised systems. This involves restricting user accounts' permissions and implementing least privilege principles to ensure that users and applications only have access to the resources and data necessary to perform their roles. Additionally, organizations can use endpoint security solutions such as host-based firewalls, intrusion detection systems (IDS), and endpoint detection and response (EDR) tools to monitor and block malicious activities on individual devices. By deploying these security controls, organizations can detect and contain incidents at the endpoint level, preventing attackers from escalating privileges or moving laterally across the network. Furthermore, organizations can deploy deception technologies to mislead attackers and divert them away from critical systems and data. Deception techniques such as honeypots, honey tokens, and decoy documents create false targets that appear attractive to attackers, leading them to reveal their presence and intentions while protecting genuine assets. Deploying deception technologies alongside other security controls can help organizations detect and contain incidents more effectively, reducing the attacker's dwell time and minimizing the impact of the breach. Incident containment also involves implementing security patches and updates promptly to address vulnerabilities exploited by attackers. Organizations should establish robust patch management processes to identify and remediate vulnerabilities in a timely manner, reducing the risk of exploitation and minimizing the impact of incidents. Automated patch management solutions can help organizations streamline the patching process by automatically deploying security updates to endpoints and infrastructure components. Additionally, organizations can leverage threat intelligence feeds and security information and event management

(SIEM) solutions to detect and respond to incidents proactively. By monitoring for indicators of compromise (IOCs) and suspicious activities, organizations can identify and contain incidents before they escalate, preventing attackers from exfiltrating data or causing further damage. Incident containment also involves communication and coordination with internal stakeholders and external partners. Organizations should establish incident response teams and communication protocols to ensure that relevant stakeholders are informed promptly and can collaborate effectively to contain and remediate incidents. This may involve notifying senior management, legal counsel, regulatory authorities, customers, and other affected parties as appropriate, following established incident response and notification procedures. Additionally, organizations can engage with external cybersecurity experts, law enforcement agencies, and incident response firms to assist with incident containment and remediation efforts. By leveraging external expertise and resources, organizations can enhance their incident response capabilities and improve their chances of containing and mitigating cybersecurity incidents effectively. Overall, effective incident containment requires a combination of technical controls, proactive monitoring, patch management, communication, and collaboration to limit the impact of incidents and protect an organization's systems, data, and reputation.

Eradicating threats from an organization's environment is a critical aspect of incident response and cybersecurity operations. One technique for eradicating threats is to identify and remove malicious files, processes, and configurations associated with the incident. This can be achieved using antivirus and antimalware tools to scan systems and identify known threats. For example, organizations can use the "antivirus" or "malware scan" command to scan files and directories for malware and quarantine or delete any malicious files detected. Additionally, organizations can leverage endpoint detection and response (EDR) solutions to conduct more detailed investigations and remediation actions on compromised endpoints. EDR tools provide real-time visibility into endpoint activity and allow security teams to identify and remediate malicious behavior quickly. Another technique for eradicating threats is to patch vulnerabilities exploited by attackers to gain unauthorized access to systems. Vulnerability management solutions can help organizations identify and prioritize vulnerabilities based on their severity and potential impact. By deploying security patches and updates promptly, organizations can close security gaps and prevent attackers from exploiting known vulnerabilities. The "patch" or "update" command can be used to install security updates on operating systems, applications, and network devices. Additionally, organizations can use network security controls such as firewalls, intrusion prevention systems (IPS), and web application firewalls (WAF) to block malicious traffic and prevent attackers from accessing vulnerable systems. By implementing strict access controls and network segmentation, organizations can limit the attacker's ability to move laterally within the network and access sensitive data or resources. Furthermore, organizations can leverage threat intelligence feeds and security information and event management (SIEM) solutions to identify and block known malicious IP addresses, domains, and URLs. By blocking malicious traffic at the network perimeter, organizations can prevent attackers from establishing command and control channels or exfiltrating data from compromised systems. Another technique for eradicating threats is to conduct thorough forensic analysis to identify the root cause of the incident and any lingering traces of malicious activity. Forensic analysis involves collecting and analyzing digital evidence from affected systems to reconstruct the timeline of events and identify the tactics, techniques, and procedures (TTPs) used by attackers. This can help organizations understand how the incident occurred and develop more effective mitigation strategies to prevent similar incidents in the future. Additionally, organizations can leverage threat hunting techniques to proactively search for signs of hidden or persistent threats within their environment. Threat hunting involves using data analytics, machine learning, and human expertise to identify anomalies and suspicious behavior that may indicate the presence of an ongoing attack. By proactively hunting for threats, organizations can identify and eradicate threats before they cause significant damage or disruption. Furthermore, organizations can leverage incident response playbooks and automated response workflows to streamline the eradication process and ensure consistent and effective response actions. Incident response playbooks provide predefined steps and procedures for responding to common types of security incidents, allowing security teams to respond quickly and decisively. Automated response workflows can help organizations orchestrate and automate remediation actions across their environment, reducing the time and effort required to eradicate threats. Overall, eradicating threats requires a combination of technical controls, proactive monitoring, patch management, forensic analysis, threat hunting, and incident response procedures to identify, contain, and remediate security incidents effectively. By implementing these techniques, organizations can strengthen their security posture and protect their systems, data, and users from cyber threats.

Chapter 6: Forensic Investigation Techniques in Incident Response

Digital forensics plays a pivotal role in incident response, providing crucial insights into the nature and scope of security incidents. It encompasses a range of techniques and methodologies aimed at collecting, analyzing, and preserving digital evidence related to cyber incidents. One fundamental aspect of digital forensics is evidence collection, which involves gathering data from various sources such as computers, servers, network devices, and mobile devices. This process requires specialized tools and techniques to ensure that the evidence is collected in a forensically sound manner, preserving its integrity and admissibility in legal proceedings. Forensic imaging tools, for example, allow investigators to create exact copies of storage media, such as hard drives and memory cards, without altering the original data. These tools use commands like "dd" or "dcfldd" to create forensic images of storage devices, ensuring that the data remains intact and unaltered during the imaging process. Once the evidence is collected, the next step in the digital forensics process is analysis, where investigators examine the collected data to uncover relevant information about the incident. This may involve searching for indicators of compromise (IOCs), such as malware artifacts, suspicious files, or anomalous network traffic. Advanced analysis techniques, such as memory forensics and malware analysis, can provide deeper insights into the tactics, techniques, and procedures (TTPs) used by attackers. Memory forensics tools, such as Volatility, allow investigators to analyze the contents of volatile memory (RAM) to identify running processes, open network connections, and other artifacts indicative of malicious activity. Similarly, malware analysis tools like IDA Pro or Ghidra enable analysts to reverse engineer malicious code to understand its functionality and behavior. These tools help investigators uncover critical details about the attack, such as the initial infection vector, the malware's capabilities, and the attacker's objectives. In addition to analyzing digital evidence, digital forensics also involves preserving the integrity of the evidence to ensure its admissibility in court. This requires following strict chain of custody procedures and documenting every step of the forensic process to demonstrate the integrity and reliability of the evidence. Chain of custody documentation includes details such as when and where the evidence was collected, who handled it, and any changes or modifications made to the evidence during the investigation. Digital forensics investigators use specialized tools, such as forensic hashing algorithms like MD5 or SHA-256, to create cryptographic hashes of digital evidence. These hashes serve as digital fingerprints, providing a unique identifier for each piece of evidence and enabling investigators to verify its integrity throughout the forensic process. Moreover, digital forensics also involves presenting findings and conclusions derived from the analysis of digital evidence in a clear and understandable manner. This often requires preparing detailed forensic reports that document the investigative process, findings, and conclusions in a format suitable for presentation to stakeholders, such as management, legal counsel, or law enforcement agencies. Forensic reports typically include an executive summary, a description of the incident, details about the evidence collected and analyzed, analysis findings, and recommendations for mitigating future incidents. Furthermore, digital forensics is an iterative process, with investigators continuously refining their techniques and methodologies to keep pace with evolving cyber threats and technologies. This involves staying updated on the latest forensic tools, techniques, and best practices through ongoing training, certifications, and participation in professional communities and forums. By continually honing their skills and expertise, digital forensics professionals can effectively contribute to the detection, investigation, and resolution of security incidents, helping organizations strengthen their cyber defenses and mitigate future risks. Conducting forensic investigations is a meticulous process that requires a systematic approach and adherence to established protocols and procedures. One of the first steps in a forensic investigation is to define the scope and objectives of the investigation, which involves understanding the nature of the incident and identifying the specific artifacts and evidence that need to be collected and analyzed. This initial phase often begins with gathering information about the incident, including details about the affected systems, networks, and users involved. Once the scope of the investigation is defined, the next step is to establish a secure and controlled environment for conducting the investigation. This typically involves setting up a dedicated forensic workstation or environment where investigators can analyze digital evidence without risk of contamination or tampering. Forensic workstations are configured with specialized tools and software designed for collecting, analyzing, and preserving digital evidence, such as disk imaging tools, file carving utilities, and memory forensics frameworks. In addition to the forensic workstation, investigators may also need access to other hardware and software resources, such as write blockers, hardware imager devices, and network monitoring tools, depending on the specific requirements of the investigation. Once the forensic environment is set up, the next phase of the investigation involves collecting digital evidence from the affected systems and networks. This process requires careful planning and execution to ensure that the evidence is collected in a forensically sound manner, preserving its integrity and admissibility in court. Disk imaging tools, such as FTK Imager or EnCase, are commonly used to create forensic images of storage devices, such as hard drives and solid-state drives (SSDs). These tools create bit-by-bit copies of the original storage media, including all data, metadata, and unallocated space, ensuring that the integrity of the evidence is maintained throughout the imaging process. Once the forensic images are acquired, investigators can begin the process of analyzing the digital evidence to uncover relevant information about the incident. This typically involves using a combination of manual and automated techniques to search for and extract artifacts from the forensic images, such as file system data, registry entries, log files, and network traffic. File carving tools, such as Scalpel or Foremost, can be used to extract files and other data structures from disk images based on their file signatures and headers. Similarly, memory forensics frameworks, like Volatility or Rekall, enable investigators to analyze the contents of volatile memory (RAM) to identify running processes, open network connections, and other artifacts indicative of malicious activity. Throughout the analysis process, investigators must maintain detailed documentation of their findings, including notes on the methodologies used, the tools employed, and any observations or insights gained from the analysis. This documentation is essential for ensuring the reproducibility and validity of the investigation and for providing a clear audit trail of the forensic process. Once the analysis is complete, investigators can begin the process of documenting their findings and preparing reports summarizing the results of the investigation. Forensic reports typically include an executive summary, a description of the incident and the investigative process, details about the evidence collected and analyzed, analysis findings, and recommendations for mitigating future incidents. These reports are often presented to stakeholders such as management, legal counsel, or law enforcement agencies and may be used as evidence in legal proceedings or regulatory investigations. In addition to conducting technical analysis of digital evidence, forensic investigators may also be called upon to provide expert testimony in court or to assist with other aspects of the legal process, such as preparing affidavits, depositions, or expert reports. This requires not only technical expertise but also effective communication skills and the ability to convey complex technical concepts in a clear and understandable manner to non-technical audiences. Moreover, conducting forensic investigations requires a thorough understanding of legal and regulatory requirements related to digital evidence collection and analysis, as well as the ability to work collaboratively with other stakeholders, such as law enforcement agencies, legal counsel, and internal or external auditors. By following established protocols and procedures and leveraging the latest tools and techniques, forensic investigators can effectively uncover and analyze digital evidence, helping organizations respond to security incidents and mitigate future risks.

Chapter 7: Incident Communication and Reporting

Communication protocols during incidents are essential for ensuring effective coordination, collaboration, and information sharing among all stakeholders involved in the incident response process. One of the key aspects of communication protocols is establishing clear lines of communication and defining roles and responsibilities for each member of the incident response team. This helps to avoid confusion and ensures that everyone knows what actions need to be taken and who is responsible for carrying them out. Additionally, communication protocols should include guidelines for how information should be communicated, including the use of formal channels such as email, chat, or phone calls, as well as informal channels such as face-to-face conversations or instant messaging platforms. These guidelines help to ensure that information is communicated in a timely and efficient manner, allowing for rapid decision-making and response to the incident. Another important aspect of communication protocols is establishing escalation procedures for escalating issues to higher levels of management or to external stakeholders such as law enforcement agencies or regulatory bodies. This ensures that critical issues are addressed promptly and that the appropriate authorities are notified as needed. Additionally, communication protocols should include provisions for documenting all communication related to the incident, including decisions made, actions taken, and any other relevant information. This documentation is important for maintaining an audit trail of the incident response process and can be valuable for post-incident analysis and reporting. Moreover, communication protocols should also address how to handle communication with external parties such as customers, vendors, partners, and the media. This may include designating specific individuals or teams to handle external communications, preparing templates for communication with external parties, and establishing guidelines for what information can be shared and how it should be communicated. Furthermore, communication protocols should include provisions for regular updates and status reports to keep all stakeholders informed about the progress of the incident response effort. This helps to maintain transparency and accountability and ensures that everyone involved in the response is kept up to date on the latest developments. Additionally, communication protocols should address how to handle communication in the event of a breach of confidentiality or sensitive information. This may include encrypting sensitive communications, restricting access to certain information to only those with a need-to-know, and implementing procedures for securely disposing of information once it is no longer needed. Furthermore, communication protocols should also address how to handle communication during different phases of the incident response process, such as detection, containment, eradication, and recovery. This may include establishing specific communication channels or workflows for each phase, as well as defining criteria for when to escalate issues or involve additional stakeholders. Moreover, communication protocols should also address how to handle communication in the event of a large-scale incident or crisis that affects multiple stakeholders or organizations. This may include establishing coordination mechanisms with other organizations or agencies involved in the response effort, as well as developing joint communication plans and protocols for sharing information and coordinating response activities. Additionally, communication protocols should include provisions for conducting post-incident communication and debriefing sessions to review the effectiveness of the response effort and identify lessons learned for future incidents. This helps to ensure continuous improvement in incident response capabilities and enhances overall preparedness for future incidents. Overall, effective communication protocols are essential for ensuring a coordinated and efficient response to security incidents, minimizing the impact of incidents, and mitigating future risks. Reporting processes for incidents play a crucial role in incident response and management, providing a structured approach for documenting, analyzing, and communicating information about security incidents within an organization. These processes typically involve a series of steps designed to capture essential details about the incident, assess its impact and severity, and communicate the necessary information to relevant stakeholders. One of the first steps in the reporting process is incident identification, where security personnel or automated monitoring systems detect unusual or suspicious activity that may indicate a security incident. Once an incident is identified, it needs to be documented promptly to ensure that all relevant Information is captured accurately. This documentation typically includes details such as the date and time of the incident, a description of the incident, the systems or assets affected, and any initial assessment of the incident's severity. Next, the incident needs to be classified based on its nature, impact, and severity. This classification helps to prioritize the response effort and allocate resources effectively. Common incident classifications include security breaches, data breaches, malware infections, denial-of-service attacks, and unauthorized access attempts. Once the incident is classified, it needs to be investigated thoroughly to determine its cause, scope, and potential impact on the organization. This investigation may involve analyzing log files, conducting forensic analysis, and interviewing relevant personnel to gather additional information about the incident. The findings of the investigation should be documented carefully to ensure that all relevant details are captured and can be used for further analysis and reporting. After the investigation is complete, the incident needs to be assessed to determine its impact on the organization's operations, systems, and data. This assessment helps to prioritize response actions and determine the appropriate level of escalation and communication. Incident impact assessments may consider factors such as the severity of the incident, the criticality of the affected systems or assets, and the potential financial or reputational damage to the organization. Based on the impact assessment, an incident response plan should be activated to address the incident effectively. This plan outlines the steps that need to be taken to contain, mitigate, and recover from the incident and specifies the roles and responsibilities of the incident response team. The incident response plan should also include provisions for communicating with internal and external stakeholders, including employees, customers, partners, regulators, and law enforcement agencies, as appropriate. Communication during incident response is essential for keeping stakeholders informed about the situation, managing expectations, and coordinating response efforts effectively. Incident response teams should use a variety of communication channels, including email, phone calls, text messages, and collaboration platforms, to ensure that information is disseminated quickly and accurately. Additionally, incident response teams should provide regular updates and status reports to keep stakeholders informed about the progress of the response effort and any changes to the situation. These updates help to maintain transparency and build trust with stakeholders, which is essential for effective incident management. As the incident response effort progresses, it is essentlal to document all response activities and decisions made during the incident. This documentation serves as an audit trail of the response process and can be valuable for post-incident analysis, reporting, and regulatory compliance purposes. Incident reports should include details such as the timeline of events, response actions taken, outcomes achieved, lessons learned, and recommendations for future improvements. Finally, after the incident has been resolved, a post-incident review should be conducted to evaluate the effectiveness of the response effort and identify areas for improvement. This review may include analyzing response metrics, soliciting feedback from stakeholders, and conducting a retrospective analysis of the incident response process. By following a structured reporting process for incidents, organizations can effectively manage and mitigate security risks, minimize the impact of incidents, and improve their overall security posture.

Chapter 8: Disaster Recovery Planning and Business Continuity

Developing disaster recovery plans is a critical aspect of organizational resilience, ensuring that businesses can continue to operate and recover quickly in the event of disruptive incidents such as natural disasters, cyberattacks, or system failures. The process of developing a disaster recovery plan typically involves several key steps designed to identify potential risks, assess their potential impact, and establish strategies and procedures for mitigating those risks and recovering from disasters. One of the first steps in developing a disaster recovery plan is to conduct a comprehensive risk assessment to identify potential threats and vulnerabilities that could disrupt business operations. This assessment may involve analyzing various factors such as the organization's geographical location, infrastructure, technology systems, and regulatory requirements to identify potential risks and their potential impact on the organization. Once potential risks have been identified, the next step is to prioritize them based on their likelihood and potential impact on the organization's operations. This prioritization helps to focus resources and attention on addressing the most critical risks first. Following the risk assessment, the organization should develop a set of disaster recovery objectives and goals that align with its overall business objectives and priorities. These objectives should be specific, measurable, achievable, relevant, and time-bound (SMART) to ensure that they are actionable and effective. With the objectives in place, the organization can then develop a detailed disaster recovery plan that outlines the strategies, procedures, and resources required to respond to and recover from various types of disasters. The disaster recovery plan should include specific procedures for each phase of the disaster recovery process, including preparation, response, recovery, and restoration. These procedures should cover various aspects such as data backup and recovery, system restoration, communications, and personnel roles and responsibilities. In addition to developing the plan itself, organizations should also establish a governance structure to oversee the implementation and maintenance of the disaster recovery plan. This governance structure may include a disaster recovery team or committee responsible for coordinating and managing the disaster recovery process, as well as defining roles and responsibilities for key personnel involved in the process. Once the disaster recovery plan has been developed and the governance structure established, the next step is to test the plan through regular exercises and drills. Testing the plan helps to identify any gaps or weaknesses in the plan and provides an opportunity to refine and improve it before an actual disaster occurs. Organizations should conduct a variety of tests, including tabletop exercises, simulations, and full-scale drills, to ensure that all aspects of the plan are thoroughly tested and validated. Additionally, organizations should review and update the disaster recovery plan regularly to reflect changes in the business environment, technology landscape, regulatory requirements, and lessons learned from previous incidents. This ongoing review and update process help to ensure that the plan remains current, relevant, and effective in mitigating the organization's risks and enabling timely recovery from disasters. In summary, developing disaster recovery plans is essential for organizations to effectively manage and mitigate the impact of disruptive incidents on their operations. By following a structured approach to developing, implementing, and testing disaster recovery plans, organizations can improve their resilience and ensure continuity of operations in the face of unforeseen challenges and disruptions. Ensuring business continuity during incidents is paramount for organizations to maintain their operations and minimize the impact of disruptions on their employees, customers, and stakeholders. One of the key strategies for ensuring business continuity during incidents is to develop a comprehensive business continuity plan (BCP) that outlines procedures and protocols for responding to and recovering from various types of incidents. The first step in developing a BCP is to conduct a thorough risk assessment to identify potential threats and vulnerabilities that could disrupt business operations. This assessment may include evaluating risks such as natural disasters, cyberattacks, pandemics, supply chain disruptions, and regulatory compliance failures. Once potential risks have been identified, the next step is to prioritize them based on their likelihood and potential impact on the organization. This prioritization helps organizations focus their resources and attention on addressing the most critical risks first. With the risks prioritized, organizations can then develop strategies and procedures for mitigating those risks and ensuring continuity of operations. These strategies may include implementing redundant systems and processes, establishing alternative work arrangements, and securing off-site backup facilities. Additionally, organizations should define roles and responsibilities for key personnel involved in the business continuity process and ensure that they are trained and prepared to respond effectively to incidents. Communication is also critical during incidents, and organizations should establish protocols for communicating with employees, customers, suppliers, and other stakeholders to keep them informed of the situation and any actions they need to take. This may include setting up communication channels such as email, phone trees, and social media platforms and providing regular updates on the status of operations and recovery efforts. Testing and exercising the BCP is another essential aspect of ensuring business continuity during incidents. Organizations should regularly conduct drills and simulations to test the effectiveness of their BCP and identify any gaps or weaknesses that need to be addressed. These exercises help to familiarize employees with their roles and responsibilities during incidents and ensure that the organization can respond quickly and effectively when a real incident occurs. In addition to developing and testing the BCP, organizations should also establish a governance structure to oversee the implementation and maintenance of the plan. This governance structure may include a business continuity team or committee responsible for coordinating and managing the business continuity process and ensuring that the plan remains current and effective. Finally, organizations should regularly review and update the BCP to reflect changes in the business environment, technology landscape, regulatory requirements, and lessons learned from previous incidents. By following these steps and implementing robust business continuity measures, organizations can minimize the impact of incidents on their operations and maintain continuity of business operations even in the face of unforeseen challenges and disruptions.

Chapter 9: Disaster Recovery Testing and Exercising

Testing disaster recovery plans is a critical aspect of ensuring organizational resilience and preparedness for potential disruptions. Organizations must conduct regular and comprehensive tests to validate the effectiveness of their disaster recovery plans and identify any gaps or weaknesses that need to be addressed. There are several testing methodologies and approaches that organizations can use to evaluate their disaster recovery plans and assess their readiness to respond to and recover from disasters. One common testing methodology is the tabletop exercise, which involves simulating a disaster scenario and walking through the steps of the disaster recovery plan with key stakeholders to identify areas for improvement. In a tabletop exercise, participants discuss and evaluate their responses to various aspects of the disaster scenario, such as communication protocols, decision-making processes, and resource allocation strategies. This type of exercise helps to identify potential challenges and bottlenecks in the disaster recovery process and allows organizations to refine their plans accordingly.

Another testing methodology is the functional exercise, which involves executing specific components of the disaster recovery plan in a controlled environment to assess their effectiveness and performance. For example, organizations may conduct a functional exercise to test their backup and recovery procedures by simulating the restoration of critical systems and data from backup media. This type of exercise helps to validate the technical aspects of the disaster recovery plan and identify any issues with the backup and recovery process that need to be addressed.

In addition to tabletop exercises and functional exercises, organizations may also conduct full-scale simulations or drills to test the entire disaster recovery plan in a real-world scenario. This type of testing involves mobilizing resources, activating emergency response procedures, and executing the entire disaster recovery plan from start to finish. Full-scale simulations are more complex and resource-intensive than tabletop exercises and functional exercises but provide a more realistic assessment of the organization's readiness to respond to and recover from disasters.

When conducting tests of disaster recovery plans, organizations should involve key stakeholders from across the organization, including IT personnel, business leaders, and other relevant departments. This ensures that all aspects of the plan are thoroughly evaluated and that any issues or concerns are addressed promptly. Additionally, organizations should document the results of the tests and develop action plans to remediate any identified weaknesses or deficiencies in the disaster recovery plan.

It's also essential for organizations to establish a regular testing schedule and conduct tests at least annually or whenever significant changes are made to the environment or the disaster recovery plan. Regular testing helps to ensure that the disaster recovery plan remains current and effective and that personnel are familiar with their roles and responsibilities during a disaster.

In addition to testing the technical aspects of the disaster recovery plan, organizations should also consider testing their communication and coordination procedures to ensure effective collaboration and decision-making during a disaster. This may involve conducting exercises to test communication channels, escalation procedures, and coordination with external partners such as vendors, suppliers, and emergency services.

Overall, testing disaster recovery plans is essential for organizations to assess their readiness to respond to and recover from disasters effectively.

By conducting regular and comprehensive tests, organizations can identify and address any weaknesses or deficiencies in their disaster recovery plans and improve their overall resilience and preparedness for potential disruptions. Conducting disaster recovery exercises is a crucial aspect of maintaining organizational resilience and preparedness in the face of potential disruptions. These exercises involve simulating various disaster scenarios to test the effectiveness of disaster recovery plans and procedures. One commonly used method for conducting disaster recovery exercises is through tabletop exercises, which are facilitated discussions where key stakeholders gather to walk through a hypothetical disaster scenario. During tabletop exercises, participants discuss their roles and responsibilities, identify potential gaps in the disaster recovery plan, and develop strategies for addressing them. These exercises provide an opportunity for organizations to evaluate their response capabilities and identify areas for improvement without the need for extensive resources or disruption to normal operations.

Another method for conducting disaster recovery exercises is through functional exercises, which involve testing specific components of the disaster recovery plan in a simulated environment. For example, organizations may conduct a functional exercise to test their backup and recovery procedures by simulating the restoration of critical systems and data from backup media. Functional exercises allow organizations to validate the technical aspects of their disaster recovery plan and identify any issues that need to be addressed. Additionally, organizations may conduct full-scale simulations or drills to test the entire disaster recovery plan in a real-world scenario. These exercises involve mobilizing resources, activating emergency response procedures, and executing the entire disaster recovery plan from start to finish.

When conducting disaster recovery exercises, it is essential to involve key stakeholders from across the organization, including IT personnel, business leaders, and other relevant departments. This ensures that all aspects of the plan are thoroughly evaluated and that any issues or concerns are addressed promptly. Additionally, organizations should document the results of the exercises and develop action plans to remediate any identified weaknesses or deficiencies in the disaster recovery plan. Regular exercises help to ensure that the disaster recovery plan remains current and effective, and that personnel are familiar with their roles and responsibilities during a disaster.

In addition to testing the technical aspects of the disaster recovery plan, organizations should also consider testing their communication and coordination procedures. This may involve conducting exercises to test communication channels, escalation procedures, and coordination with external partners such as vendors, suppliers, and emergency services. Effective communication is critical during a disaster, and testing communication procedures helps to ensure that information flows smoothly between all stakeholders involved in the response effort.

Overall, conducting disaster recovery exercises is essential for organizations to assess their readiness to respond to and recover from disasters effectively. By regularly testing their disaster recovery plans and procedures, organizations can identify and address any weaknesses or deficiencies, improve their overall resilience, and minimize the impact of potential disruptions on their operations.

Chapter 10: Advanced Incident Response and Recovery Strategies

Advanced incident response tactics encompass a range of strategies and techniques employed by cybersecurity professionals to detect, contain, and remediate sophisticated cyber threats and attacks. These tactics go beyond the basic incident response procedures and require a deep understanding of cybersecurity principles, threat intelligence, and advanced technical skills. One advanced tactic often utilized in incident response is the use of threat hunting, which involves proactively searching for signs of malicious activity or compromise within an organization's network. Threat hunters leverage various tools and techniques to identify indicators of compromise (IOCs) and anomalous behavior that may indicate a security breach.

To conduct threat hunting effectively, security teams often use specialized tools such as intrusion detection systems (IDS), security information and event management (SIEM) platforms, and endpoint detection and response (EDR) solutions. These tools help analysts collect and correlate large volumes of data from across the network, allowing them to identify potential threats and investigate suspicious activity further. Additionally, threat hunters may utilize threat intelligence feeds and open-source intelligence (OSINT) to stay informed about emerging threats and attack trends, enabling them to better anticipate and respond to potential security incidents.

Another advanced tactic in incident response is the use of deception technology, which involves deploying decoy systems, networks, or data to lure attackers into revealing their presence and tactics. Deception technology can help organizations detect and deflect attacks in real-time, providing valuable insights into the techniques and tools used by adversaries. By deploying decoys strategically throughout their network, organizations can create a more challenging environment for attackers to navigate, increasing the likelihood of detection and reducing the risk of successful compromise.

In addition to threat hunting and deception technology, incident responders may also employ advanced forensic techniques to analyze and attribute cyber attacks. Forensic analysis involves collecting and analyzing digital evidence from compromised systems to determine the root cause of an incident, identify the attacker's motives and tactics, and gather intelligence to prevent future attacks. This may include analyzing network traffic logs, examining file system artifacts, and conducting memory and disk forensics to reconstruct the timeline of events leading up to and following the incident.

Furthermore, incident responders may utilize advanced incident response playbooks and automation tools to streamline their response efforts and improve their overall efficiency. Playbooks outline predefined response procedures and workflows for different types of security incidents, allowing responders to quickly assess the situation and execute the appropriate response actions. Automation tools can help automate repetitive tasks, such as data collection, analysis, and remediation, allowing responders to focus their time and expertise on more complex and high-priority tasks.

Moreover, collaboration and information sharing with other organizations and industry peers are essential components of advanced incident response tactics. By participating in information sharing and threat intelligence sharing initiatives, organizations can gain valuable insights into emerging threats and attack techniques, allowing them to better prepare and respond to potential security incidents. Additionally, collaboration with law enforcement agencies and cybersecurity organizations can help facilitate the investigation and attribution of cyber attacks, leading to the identification and prosecution of cyber criminals.

Overall, advanced incident response tactics play a crucial role in helping organizations detect, respond to, and recover from sophisticated cyber threats and attacks. By leveraging threat hunting, deception technology, forensic analysis, automation, and collaboration, organizations can enhance their incident response capabilities and better protect their sensitive data and assets from evolving cyber threats. Innovative approaches to incident recovery involve the exploration and implementation of novel strategies and technologies to restore systems and operations following a cybersecurity incident. These approaches are essential in modern cybersecurity practices, as organizations face increasingly sophisticated and disruptive cyber threats that can cause significant damage to their infrastructure, data, and reputation. One innovative approach to incident recovery is the use of immutable infrastructure, which involves designing systems and applications in a way that prevents unauthorized changes or modifications. By leveraging technologies such as containerization and infrastructure as code (IaC), organizations can create immutable environments where changes are made through code and deployed automatically, reducing the risk of configuration drift and unauthorized access.

Immutable infrastructure can also simplify incident recovery efforts by enabling organizations to roll back to a known, secure state in the event of a security breach or compromise. Additionally, organizations can use version control systems such as Git to track changes to their infrastructure code and quickly identify and revert any unauthorized modifications. Another innovative approach to incident recovery is the use of cloud-based disaster recovery solutions, which leverage the scalability and flexibility of cloud computing to provide resilient and cost-effective data protection and recovery capabilities.

Cloud-based disaster recovery solutions allow organizations to replicate their critical systems and data to off-site cloud environments, providing redundancy and failover capabilities in the event of a disaster or outage. By leveraging cloud infrastructure and services, organizations can quickly recover from incidents and minimize downtime, ensuring business continuity and maintaining customer trust. Moreover, cloud-based disaster recovery solutions offer automatic failover and failback capabilities, allowing organizations to seamlessly transition between their primary and secondary environments without manual intervention.

Furthermore, organizations can implement advanced data protection and recovery techniques such as continuous data protection (CDP) and point-in-time recovery (PITR) to enhance their incident recovery capabilities. CDP solutions capture and replicate changes to data in real-time, allowing organizations to recover to any point in time with minimal data loss. PITR solutions enable organizations to restore their systems and data to specific points in time, providing granular recovery capabilities and ensuring data integrity and consistency.

In addition to technological innovations, organizations can also adopt proactive incident recovery strategies such as cyber resilience and business continuity planning. Cyber resilience involves designing systems and processes to withstand and recover from cyber attacks and disruptions effectively. By integrating security controls, incident response procedures, and recovery mechanisms into their operations, organizations can minimize the impact of incidents and maintain essential business functions.

Moreover, organizations can conduct regular risk assessments and scenario-based exercises to identify potential threats and vulnerabilities and validate their incident recovery plans. By simulating various incident scenarios, organizations can evaluate the effectiveness of their response procedures, identify gaps and weaknesses, and refine their incident recovery strategies accordingly. Additionally, organizations can leverage threat intelligence and information sharing initiatives to stay informed about emerging threats and attack trends, enabling them to better prepare for and respond to potential incidents.

Overall, innovative approaches to incident recovery are essential for organizations to effectively respond to and recover from cybersecurity incidents. By leveraging technologies such as immutable infrastructure, cloud-based disaster recovery solutions, and advanced data protection techniques, organizations can enhance their incident recovery capabilities and minimize the impact of incidents on their operations and stakeholders. Additionally, proactive strategies such as cyber resilience and business continuity planning are crucial for ensuring the resilience and continuity of business operations in the face of evolving cyber threats and challenges.

Conclusion

In summary, the "CISM Exam Pass" book bundle offers a comprehensive and structured approach to preparing for the Certified Information Security Manager (CISM) exam. Across the four books included in this bundle, readers have gained a deep understanding of foundational principles and concepts, mastered risk management techniques, explored advanced strategies for governance and compliance, and learned expert techniques for incident response and disaster recovery.

Book 1, "CISM Exam Prep: Foundation Principles and Concepts," serves as an essential starting point for aspiring CISM professionals, providing a solid foundation in the core principles and concepts of information security management. Readers have learned about the key domains of the CISM exam, including information security governance, risk management, information security program development and management, and incident management. By mastering the foundational concepts outlined in this book, readers have laid the groundwork for success in their CISM exam journey.

Book 2, "Mastering Risk Management in Information Security for CISM," delves deep into the intricacies of risk management in the context of information security. Readers have explored various risk assessment methodologies, learned how to identify and prioritize risks, and gained insights into developing effective risk mitigation strategies. Through real-world examples and practical exercises, readers have honed their risk management skills and prepared themselves to tackle risk-related questions on the CISM exam with confidence.

Book 3, "Advanced Strategies for Governance and Compliance in CISM," takes readers beyond the basics of information security governance and compliance, providing advanced strategies for effectively managing governance frameworks and navigating complex regulatory landscapes. Readers have learned about emerging trends and best practices in governance, compliance, and privacy, empowering them to develop robust governance frameworks and ensure compliance with regulatory requirements.

Book 4, "Expert Techniques for Incident Response and Disaster Recovery in CISM," equips readers with the knowledge and skills needed to effectively respond to and recover from cybersecurity incidents and disasters. Readers have learned about incident response methodologies, explored advanced forensic techniques, and gained insights into developing comprehensive disaster recovery plans. Armed with expert techniques and strategies, readers are prepared to handle incidents and disasters with agility and precision, minimizing disruption to business operations and safeguarding organizational assets.

Collectively, the books in the "CISM Exam Pass" bundle provide a comprehensive study guide for aspiring CISM professionals, covering the breadth and depth of topics needed to succeed in the CISM exam and excel in the field of information security management. Whether readers are looking to enhance their knowledge, advance their careers, or obtain professional certification, this bundle serves as an invaluable resource and guide on their journey towards becoming Certified Information Security Managers.

www.ingramcontent.com/pod-product-compliance
Lightning Source LLC
Chambersburg PA
CBHW071233050326
40690CB00011B/2102